Francis Beau

John Fletcher

Rule a Wife and Have a Wife

Elibron Classics
www.elibron.com

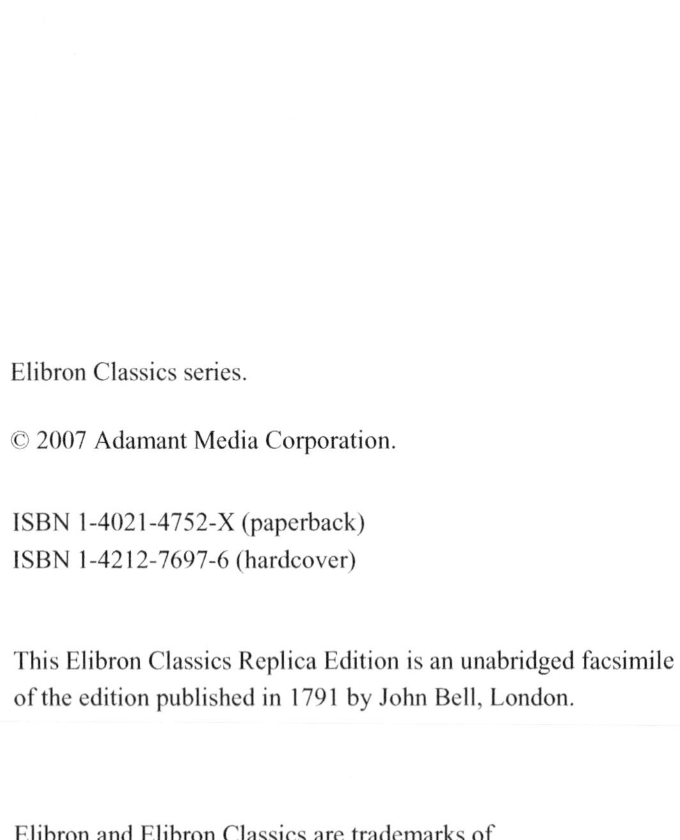

Elibron Classics series.

ISBN 1-4021-4752-X (paperback)
ISBN 1-4212-7697-6 (hardcover)

This Elibron Classics Replica Edition is an unabridged facsimile of the edition published in 1791 by John Bell, London.

RULE A WIFE AND HAVE A WIFE.

Estif. And here's a chain of Whitings eyes for pearls
A Musselmonger would have made a better.

Act II. RULE A WIFE AND HAVE A WIFE. Scene II.

De Wilde ad vir. pinx! Thornthwaite sculp.

Mr. LEWIS as the COPPER CAPTAIN,

Alas, I am a fellow of no reckoning!
Nor worth a lady's eye.

London. Printed for J. Bell, British Library, Strand, April 27. 1791.

RULE A WIFE

AND

HAVE A WIFE.

A

COMEDY.

By BEAUMONT AND FLETCHER.

ADAPTED FOR

THEATRICAL REPRESENTATION,

AS PERFORMED AT THE

THEATRES-ROYAL

DRURY-LANE AND COVENT-GARDEN.

REGULATED FROM THE PROMPT-BOOK,

By Permission of the Managers.

"The Lines distinguished by inverted Commas, are omitted in the Representation."

LONDON:

Printed for the Proprietors, under the Direction of
JOHN BELL, British-Library, STRAND,
Bookseller to His Royal Highness the PRINCE of WALES.

M DCC XCI.

FRANCIS BEAUMONT
AND
JOHN FLETCHER.

BEAUMONT and FLETCHER, those twin stars that run
Their glorious course round SHAKSPERE's golden sun.

IT has seldom happened, that so perfect a parallel has been seen, as that which these friendly and illustrious Bards exhibited, in their births, minds, and accomplishments. By birth they were alike illustrious, for the father of BEAUMONT was a Judge of the Common Pleas, and the parent of FLETCHER arrived to the dignity of the Bishopric of London.—Mentally their gifts were so similar, that it were indeed a fruitless labour for curiosity to attempt a discrimination of their blended labours.--They both, too, possessed that fashionable ease, and sprightly fancy, which so considerably polish life; and the *first* and *best* was the only company they frequented.

THE year of FLETCHER's birth was 1576—that of BEAUMONT's 1585. The latter died in

1615—the former lived nearly the same time after him as he had lived before him, for his death happened during the plague of 1625.

How that complete co-operation of design and execution, that is visible in their works was effected, there are now no means of ascertaining;—but we are given to understand, traditionally, that the fancy of FLETCHER was fertile even to luxuriance, and that BEAUMONT possessed most of the restraining severity of judgment—that BEAUMONT regulated the plots, and that FLETCHER rapidly furnished out the dialogue———that FLETCHER had most *wit*, and BEAUMONT most *thought*.—Equally gifted otherways, holding frequent conferences together, with souls that were perfectly congenial, the difficulty was soon done away, and it is probable, that the collision of these Wits might stimulate an activity which solitude is apt to dull, and invigorate the minds that began to stagnate when they were sundered.—They produced the following amazing list of Dramatic Works:

The Woman Hater —	1607	*Cupid's Revenge* —	1615
Masque of the Inner Temple and Grays Inn —	1612	*The Scornful Lady* —	1616
The Knight of the Burning Pestle — —	1613	*The King and no King*	1619
		The Maid's Tragedy	1619
		Thierry and Theodoret	1621

Philaster — —	1622	*Wit without Money* —	1639
The Faithful Shepherdess		*Rollo* — — —	1639
The Two Noble Kinsmen	1634	*Rule a Wife and have a Wife* — — —	1640
The Elder Brother —	1637		
Monsieur Thomas —	1638	*The Night Walker* —	1640

The following 34 Plays were first published together in 1647.

The Mad Lover
The Spanish Curate
The Little French Lawyer
The Custom of the Country
The Noble Gentleman
The Captain
The Beggar's Bush
The Coxcomb
The False One
The Chances
The Loyal Subject
The Laws of Candy
The Lover's Progress
The Island Princess
The Humorous Lieutenant
The Nice Valour
The Maid in the Mill
The Prophetess
Bonduca
The Sea Voyage
The Double Marriage
The Pilgrim
The Knight of Malta
The Woman's Prize
Love's Cure
The Honest Man's Fortune
The Queen of Corinth
Women pleased
A Wife for a Month
Wit at several Weapons
Valentinian
The Fair Maid of the Inn
Love's Pilgrimage
Four Plays in One

The Wild Goose Chase 1679
The Widow — — 1652
The Jeweller of Amsterdam; or, *The Hague*
The Faithful Friend
A Right Woman
The History of Mador King of Britain

RULE A WIFE AND HAVE A WIFE.

THE piece now to be charaсterized has ever been a favourite, and perhaps deservedly will continue to be so—for though the fable be improbable, and much of the sentiment prurient, yet most of the thoughts will stand upon the bases of truth and nature.

OF SHAKSPERE's school, the language seems similar with his—It discovers the want of grammar remarkable in the writings of that age—it discovers also that pregnant power of expression which no other age has equalled.

THIS play interests variously and oddly——LEON and PEREZ are comic perfection. In modern representation, from the delight attached to female performances, ESTIFANIA is thought the principal character; but the fact is, she occasions comic situation rather than constitutes it:—if she *did* no more than she *says*, she would be dismissed with little favour or affection.

CACAFOGO is a creation of the Poet, for Nature never formed a combination of beastly *gluttony* and griping *avarice*—The characters never have been, it is believed, or will be, otherwise than dramatically compounded.

PROLOGUE.

PLEASURE attend ye, and about ye sit
The springs of mirth, fancy, delight, and wit,
To stir you up; do not your looks let fall,
Nor to remembrance our late errors call,
Because this day we're Spaniards all again;
The story of our play, and our scene Spain:
The errors, too, do not for this cause hate,
Now we present their wit, and not their state.
Nor, ladies, be not angry, if you see
A young fresh beauty wanton, and too free,
Seek to abuse her husband, still 'tis Spain;
No such gross errors in your kingdom reign:
You're Vestals all, and though we blow the fire,
We seldom make it flame up to desire:
Take no example neither to begin,
For some by precedent delight to sin;
Nor blame the poet if he slip aside
Sometimes lasciviously, if not too wide.
But hold your fans close, and then smile at ease;
A cruel scene did never lady please.
For, gentlemen, pray be not you displeas'd,
Though we present some men fool'd, some diseas'd,
Some drunk, some mad; we mean not you, you're free,
We tax no farther than our comedy,
You are our friends, sit noble, then, and see.

Dramatis Personae.

DRURY-LANE.

	Men.
DUKE of MEDINA - - - -	Mr. Barrymore.
DON JUAN DE CASTRO, *a Spanish Colonel*	Mr. Packer.
SANCHIO, } *Officers in the Army* -	Mr. Phillimore.
ALONZO, } -	Mr. R. Palmer.
MICHAEL PEREZ, *the Copper Captain* -	Mr. Palmer.
LEON, *Brother to* Altea, *and by her contrivance married to* Margaritta - -	Mr. Kemble.
CACAFOGO, *a rich Usurer* - - -	Mr. Moody.
	Women.
MARGARITTA, *a wanton Lady, married to* Leon, *by whom she is reclaimed* - -	Mrs. Ward.
ALTEA, *her Servant* - - - -	Miss Tidswell.
CLARA, *a Spanish Lady* - - -	Miss Barnes.
ESTIFANIA, *a Woman of intrigue* - -	Miss Farren.
An Old Woman - - - -	Mr. Baddeley.
Maid - - - - - -	Mrs. Waldron.

COVENT-GARDEN.

	Men.
DUKE of MEDINA - - - -	Mr. Macready.
DON JUAN DE CASTRO, *a Spanish Colonel*	Mr. Davies.
SANCHIO, } *Officers in the Army* -	Mr. Thompson.
ALONZO, } -	Mr. Powell.
MICHAEL PEREZ, *the Copper Captain* -	Mr. Lewis.
LEON, *Brother to* Altea, *and by her contrivance married to* Margaritta - -	Mr. Holman.
CACAFOGO, *a rich Usurer* - - -	Mr. Cubit.
	Women.
MARGARITTA, *a wanton Lady, married to* Leon, *by whom she is reclaimed* -	Mrs. Bernard.
ALTEA, *her Servant* - - -	Miss Stewart.
CLARA, *a Spanish Lady* . - -	Miss Platt.
ESTIFANIA, *a Woman of intrigue* - -	Mrs. Abington.
An Old Woman - - - -	Mr. Quick.
Maid - - - - - - -	Miss Painter.

Visiting Ladies. SCENE, Spain.

RULE A WIFE

AND

HAVE A WIFE.

ACT I. SCENE I.

A Chamber. *Enter* DON JUAN DE CASTRO *and* MICHAEL PEREZ.

Michael.

ARE your companies full, Colonel?

Juan. No, not yet, sir.
Nor will not be this month yet, as I reckon.
How rises your command?

Mich. We pick up still,
And as our monies hold out, we have men come.
About that time, I think, we shall be full too:
Many young gallants go.

Juan. And unexperienc'd.
" The wars are dainty dreams to young hot spirits;
" Time and experience will allay those visions.
" We have strange things to fill our numbers:"
There's one Don Leon, a strange goodly fellow,

Commended to me from some noble friends,
For my Alferes.

Mich. I've heard of him, and that he hath serv'd before too.

Juan. But no harm done, not ever meant, Don Michael,
That came to my ears yet: ask him a question,
He blushes like a girl, and answers little,
To the point less. "He wears a sword, a good one,
" And good cloaths too; he's whole skinn'd, has no hurt yet; 21
" Good promising hopes." I never yet heard certainly,
Of any gentleman that saw him angry.

Mich. Preserve him, he'll conclude a peace if need be;
Many as stout as he will go along with us,
That swear as valiantly as heart can wish.
Their mouths charg'd with six oaths at once, and whole ones,
That make the drunken Dutch creep into mole-hills.

Juan. 'Tis true, such we must look for. But, Michael Perez,
When heard you of Donna Margaritta, the great heiress?

Mich. I hear every hour of her, though I ne'er saw her;
She is the main discourse. Noble Don Juan de Castro,
How happy were that man could catch this wench up,
And live at ease! She's fair and young, and wealthy,

Infinite wealthy, and as gracious too
In all her entertainments, as men report.

Juan. But she is proud, sir, that I know for certain,
And that comes seldom without wantonness:
He that shall marry her, must have a rare hand.

Mich. Would I were married; I would find that wisdom,
With a light rein to rule my wife. If e'er woman
Of the most subtile mould went beyond me,
I'd give boys leave to hoot me out o' the parish.

Enter Servant.

Ser. Sir, there be two gentlewomen attend to speak with you.

Juan. Wait on 'em in.

Mich. Are they two handsome women?

Ser. They seem so, very handsome; but they're veil'd, sir.

Mich. Thou puttest sugar in my mouth. How it melts with me!
I love a sweet young wench.

Juan. Wait on them in, I say. [*Exit Servant.*

Mich. Don Juan.

Juan. Michael, how you burnish?
Will not this soldier's heat out of your bones yet?

Mich. There be two.

Juan. Say honest, what shame have you then?

Mich. I would fain see that;
I've been in the Indies twice, and have seen strange things;

But for two honest women:——one I read at once.
Juan. Pr'ythee, be modest.
Mich. I'll be any thing.

Enter Servant, DONNA CLARA, *and* ESTIFANIA *veiled.*

Juan. You're welcome, ladies.
Mich. Both hooded! I like 'em well though:
They came not for advice in law sure hither:
" May be they'd learn to raise the pike; I'm for 'em."
They're very modest; 'tis a fine preludium.
Juan. With me, or with this gentleman, would you speak, lady?
Cla. With you, sir, as I guess, Juan de Castro.
Mich. Her curtain opens; she is a pretty gentle-woman.
Juan. I am the man, and shall be bound to fortune,
I may do any service to your beauties.
Cla. Captain, I hear you're marching down to Flanders,
To serve the Catholic king.
Juan. I am, sweet lady.
Cla. I have a kinsman, and a noble friend,
Employ'd in those wars; may be, sir, you know him;
Don Campusano, captain of carbines,
To whom I would request your nobleness
To give this poor remembrance. [*Gives a letter.*
Juan. I shall do it:
I know the gentleman, a most worthy captain.
Cla. Something in private.

Juan. Step aside: I'll serve thee.
[*Exeunt* Juan *and* Clara.

Mich. Pr'ythee, let me see thy face.

Estif. Sir, you must pardon me;
Women of our sort, that maintain fair memories,
And keep suspect off from their chastities,
Had need wear thicker veils.

Mich. I am no blaster of a lady's beauty,
Nor bold intruder on her special favours:
I know how tender reputation is,
And with what guards it ought to be preserv'd.
Lady, you may to me——

Estif. You must excuse me, Signior, I come
Not here to sell myself.

Mich. As I'm a gentleman; by the honour of a soldier.

Estif. I believe you,——
I pray be civil: I believe you'd see me,
And when you've seen me, I believe you'll like me;
But in a strange place, to a stranger too,
As if I came on purpose to betray you,
Indeed I will not.

Mich. I shall love you dearly,
And 'tis a sin to fling away affection;
I have no mistress; no desire to honour
Any but you.
I know not, you have struck me with your modesty
So deep, and taken from me
All the desire I might bestow on others——
Quickly before they come.

Estif. Indeed I dare not.
But since I see you're so desirous, sir,
To view a poor face that can merit nothing
But your repentance——
Mich. It must needs be excellent.
Estif. And with what honesty you ask it of me,
When I am gone let your man follow me,
And view what house I enter. Thither come,
For there I dare be bold to appear open ;
And as I like your virtuous carriage, then

Enter JUAN, CLARA, *and Servant.*

I shall be able to give welcome to you.
She hath done her business, I must take my leave, sir.
Mich. I'll kiss your fair white hand, and thank you, lady.
My man shall wait, and I shall be your servant.
Sirrah, come near, hark.
Ser. I shall do it faithfully. [*Exit.*
Juan. You will command me no more services ?
Cla. To be careful of your noble health, dear sir,
That I may ever honour you.
Juan. I thank you,
And kiss your hands. Wait on the ladies down there.
[*Exeunt Ladies and Servant.*
Mich. You had the honour to see the face that came to you ?
Juan. And 'twas a fair one. What was yours, Don Michael ?

Mich. Mine was i'th'eclipse, and had a cloud drawn over it.
But I believe well, and I hope 'tis handsome.
She had a hand would stir a holy hermit.
Juan. You know none of 'em?
Mich. No.
Juan. Then I do, Captain;
But I'll say nothing till I see the proof on't.
Sit close, Don Perez, or your worship's caught.
Mich. Were those she brought love letters?
Juan. A packet to a kinsman now in Flanders.
Yours was very modest, methought.
Mich. Some young unmanaged thing:
But I may live to see.
Juan, 'Tis worth experience.
Let's walk abroad and view our companies. [*Exeunt.*

SCENE II.

" *A Street.* *Enter* SANCHIO *and* ALONZO.

" *San.* What, are you for the wars, Alonzo?
" *Alon.* It may be ay,
" It may be no, e'en as the humour takes me.
" If I find peace among the female creatures,
" And easy entertainment, I'll stay at home.
" I'm not so far oblig'd yet to long marches
" And mouldy biscuits, to run mad for honour.
" When you're all gone, I have my choice before me.

" *San.* Ay, of which hospital thou'lt sweat in: wilt
" Thou never leave whoring?
" *Alon.* There is less danger in't than gunning, Sanchio.
" Tho' we be shot sometimes, the shot's not mortal;
" Besides, it breaks no limbs.
" *San.* But it disables 'em.
" Dost see how thou pullest thy legs after thee,
" As if they hung by points?
" *Alon.* Better to pull 'em thus, than walk on wooden ones;
" Serve bravely for a billet to support me.
" *San.* Fie, fie, 'tis base.
" *Alon.* Dost count it base to suffer?
" Suffer abundantly? 'Tis the crown of honour.
" You think it nothing to lie twenty days
" Under a surgeon's hand that has no mercy.
" *San.* As thou hast done, I'm sure: but I perceive now
" Why you desire to stay; the orient heiress,
" The Margaritta, sir.
" *Alon.* I would I had her.
" *San.* They say she'll marry.
" *Alon.* Yes, I think she will.
" *San.* And marry suddenly, as report goes, too.
" She fears her youth will not hold out, Alonzo.
" *Alon.* I would I had the sheathing on't.
" *San.* They say too,
" She has a greedy eye, that must be fed
" With more than one man's meat.

" *Alon.* Would she were mine,
" I'd cater for her well enough: but, Sanchio,
" There be too many great men that adore her;
" Princes, and princes' fellows, that claim privilege.
" *San.* Yet those stand off i'the way of marriage;
" To be tied to a man's pleasure is a second labour.
" *Alon.* She has bought a brave house here in town.
" *San.* I've heard so.
" *Alon.* If she convert it now to pious uses,
" And bid poor gentlemen welcome.
" *San.* When comes she to it?
" *Alon.* Within these two days: she's in the country yet,
" And keeps the noblest house.
" *San.* Then there's some hope of her.
" Wilt thou go my way?
" *Alon.* No, no, I must leave you,
" And repair to an old gentlewoman that
" Has credit with her, that can speak a good word.
" *San.* Send thee good fortune, but make thy body sound first.
" *Alon.* I am a soldier,
" And too sound a body becomes me not;
" So farewell, Sanchio. [*Exeunt.*"

SCENE III.

Another Street, ESTIFANIA *crosses the Stage. Enter a Servant of* MICHAEL PEREZ *after her.*

Ser. 'Tis this or that house, or I've lost my aim;
They're both fair buildings;—she walk'd plaguy fast.

Enter ESTIFANIA, *courtesies, and exit.*

And hereabouts I lost her. Stay, that's she;
'Tis very she;——she makes me a low court'sy:——
Let me note the place, the street I well remember.
[*Exeunt.*

SCENE IV.

A Chamber in Margaritta's *House. Enter three old Ladies.*

1 *Lady.* What should it mean, that in such haste
we're sent for?

2 *Lady.* Belike the Lady Margaret has some
business
She'd break to us in private.

3 *Lady.* It should seem so.
'Tis a good lady, and a wise young lady.

2 *Lady.* And virtuous enough too, that I warrant ye,
For a young woman of her years: 'tis a pity
To load her tender age with too much virtue.

3 *Lady*, 'Tis more sometimes than we can well away with.

Enter ALTEA.

Alt. Good-morrow, ladies.
All. 'Morrow, my good madam.
1 *Lady.* How does the sweet young beauty, lady Margaret?
2 *Lady.* Has she slept well after her walk last night?
1 *Lady.* Are her dreams gentle to her mind?
Alt. All's well,
She's very well: she sent for you thus suddenly,
To give her counsel in a business
That much concerns her.
2 *Lady.* She does well and wisely,
" To ask the counsel of the ancient'st. Madam,
" Our years have run through many things she knows not."
Alt. She would fain marry.
1 *Lady.* 'Tis a proper calling,
And well beseems her years. Who would she yoke with?
Alt. That's left to argue on. I pray come in
And break your fast; drink a good cup or two,
To strengthen your understandings, then she'll tell ye.
2 *Lady.* And good wine breeds good counsel, we'll yield to ye. [*Exeunt.*

SCENE V.

A Street. *Enter* JUAN DE CASTRO *and* LEON.

Juan. Have you seen any service?
Leon. Yes.
Juan. Where:
Leon. Every where.
Juan. What office bore ye?
Leon. None, I was not worthy.
Juan. What captains know you?
Leon. None, they were above me.
Juan. Were you ne'er hurt?
Leon. Not that I well remember;
But once I stole a hen, and then they beat me.
Pray ask me no long questions. I've an ill memory.
Juan. This is an ass. Did you ne'er draw your sword yet?
Leon. Not to do any harm, I thank Heav'n for't.
Juan. Nor ne'er ta'en prisoner?
Leon. No, I ran away;
For I ne'er had no money to redeem me.
Juan. Can you endure a drum?
Leon. It makes my head ach.
Juan. Are you not valiant when you're drunk?
Leon. I think not; but I am loving, Sir.
Juan. What a lump is this man!
Was your father wise?
Leon. Too wise for me, I'm sure;
For he gave all he had to my younger brother.

Juan. That was no foolish part, I'll bear you witness.
Canst thou lie with a woman?

Leon. I think I could make shift, Sir;
But I am bashful.

Juan. In the night?

Leon. I know not.
Darkness indeed may do some good upon me.

Juan. Why art thou sent to me to be my officer,
Ay, and commended too, when thou dar'st not fight?

Leon. There be more officers of my opinion,
Or I'm cozen'd, Sir; men that talk more too.

Juan. How wilt thou 'scape a bullet?

Leon. Why, by chance.
They aim at honourable men; alas, I'm none, Sir.

Juan. This fellow hath some doubts in his talk that strike me.

Enter ALONZO.

He cannot be all fool. Welcome, Alonzo.

Alon. What have you got there, Temperance into your company?
The spirit of peace? we shall have wars by the ounce then.

Enter CACAFOGO.

Oh, here's another pumpion, the cramm'd son of a starv'd usurer, Cacafogo.
Both their brains butter'd, cannot make two spoonfuls.

Caca. My father's dead, I am a man of war too,
Monies, demesnes; I've ships at sea too, captains.

Juan. Take heed o' the Hollanders, your ships may leak else.

Caca. I scorn the Hollanders, there are my drunkards.

Alon. Put up your gold, sir, I will borrow it else.

Caca. I'm satisfied you shall not.
Come out, I know thee, meet mine anger instantly.

Leon. I never wrong'd ye.

Caca. Thou'st wrong'd mine honour,
Thou look'st upon my mistress thrice laciviously,
I'll make it good.

Juan. Do not heat yourself, you will surfeit.

Caca. Thou want'st my money too, with a pair of base bones,
In whom there was no truth for which I beat thee,
I beat thee much; now I will hurt thee dangerously.
This shall provoke thee. [*He strikes.*

" *Alon* You struck too low, by a foot sir.

" *Juan.* You must get a ladder, when you would beat this fellow.

Leon. I cannot chuse but kick again; pray, pardon me.

Caca. Hadst thou not ask'd my pardon, I had kill'd thee.
I leave thee, as a thing despis'd, *baso las manos a vostra Seignora.* [*Exit* Caca.

Alon. You've 'scap'd by miracles, there is not in all Spain,
A spirit of more fury than this fire-drake.

Leon. I see he's hasty, and I'd give him leave

To beat me soundly, if he'd take my bond.
Juan. What shall I do with this fellow?
Alon. Turn him off,
He will infect the camp with cowardice,
If he go with thee.
Juan. About some week hence, sir,
If I can hit upon no abler officer,
You shall hear from me.
Leon. I desire no better. [*Exeunt.*

SCENE VI.

A Chamber in MARGARITTA'S *House. Enter* ESTIFANIA *and* PEREZ.

Per. You've made me now too bountiful amends, Lady,
For your strict carriage when you saw me first.
These beauties were not meant to be conceal'd;
It was a wrong to hide so sweet an object;
I could now chide ye, but it shall be thus:
No other anger ever touch your sweetness,
Estif. Y' appear to me so honest and so civil,
Without a blush, sir, I dare bid you welcome.
Per. Now, let me ask your name.
Estif. 'Tis Estifania, the heir of this poor place.
Per. Poor, do you call it?
There's nothing that I cast mine eyes upon,
But shews both rich and admirable; all the rooms

Are hung as if a princess were to dwell here;
The gardens, orchards, every thing so curious.
Is all that plate your own too?
Estif. 'Tis but little,
Only for present use; I've more and richer,
When need shall call, or friends compel me use it;
The suits you see of all the upper chambers,
Are those that commonly adorn the house;
I think I have besides, as fair as Seville,
Or any town in Spain, can parallel.
Per. Now if she be not married, I have some hopes.
Are you a maid?
Estif. You make me blush to answer;
I ever was accounted so to this hour,
And that's the reason that I live retir'd, sir.
Per. Then would I counsel you to marry presently,
(If I can get her I am made for ever) [*Aside.*
For every year you lose, you lose a beauty.
A husband now, an honest, careful husband,
Were such a comfort. Will ye walk above stairs?
Estif. This place will fit our talk, 'tis fitter far, sir;
Above there are day-beds, and such temptations
I dare not trust, sir.
Per. She's excellent wise withal, too.
Estif. You nam'd a husband; I am not so strict, sir,
Nor ty'd unto a virgin's solitariness,
But if an honest, and a noble one,
Rich, and a soldier, for so I've vow'd he shall be,
Were offer'd me, I think I should accept him.
But above all, he must love.

Per. He were base else.
There's comfort ministred in the word soldier.
How sweetly should I live!
Estif. I'm not so ignorant,
But that I know well how to be commanded,
And how again to make myself obey'd, sir.
I waste but little? I have gather'd much:
My rial not less worth when it is spent,
If spent by my direction. To please my husband,
I hold it as indifferent in my duty,
To be his maid i' th' kitchen, or his cook,
As in the hall to know myself the mistress.
Per. Sweet, rich, and provident; now, fortune, stick to me.
I am a soldier, and a bachelor, lady;
And such a wife as you I could love infinitely.
They that use many words, some are deceitful:
I long to be a husband, and a good one;
For 'tis most certain I shall make a precedent
For all that follow me, to love their ladies.
I'm young, you see, able I'd have you think too;
If 't please you know, try me before you take me.
'Tis true, I shall not meet in equal wealth with ye;
But jewels, chains, such as the war has given me,
A thousand ducats too in ready gold,
As rich clothes, too, as any he bears arms, lady.
Estif. You're a gentleman, and fair, I see by ye,
And such a man I'd rather take——
Per. Pray do so.
I'll have a priest o' the sudden.

Estif. And as suddenly
You will repent too.

Per. I'll be hang'd or drown'd first,
By this, and this, and this kiss.

Estif. You're a flatterer,
But I must say there was something when I saw you
First, in that noble face, that stirred my fancy.

Per. I'll stir it better ere you sleep, sweet lady.
I'll send for all my trunks, and give up all to ye,
Into your own dispose, before I bed ye;
And then, sweet wench.

Estif. You have the art to cozen me.

[*Exeunt.*

ACT II. SCENE I.

An Apartment in Margaritta's House. Enter MARGARITTA, *three Ladies, and* ALTEA.

Margaritta.

COME in, and give me your opinions seriously.

1 *Lady.* You say you have a mind to marry, lady.

Mar. 'Tis true, I have, for to preserve my credit,
" Yet not so much for that, as to preserve my state, ladies.
" Conceive me right, there lies the main o' th' question:
" Credit I can redeem, money will imp it;
" But when my money's gone, when the law shall

" Seize that, and for incontinency, strip me
" Of all.

" 1 *Lady*. Do you find your body so malicious that way ?

" *Mar*. I find it as all bodies are, that are young and lusty,
" Lazy, and high fed."
I desire my pleasure, and pleasure I must have.

2 *Lady*. 'Tis fit you should have,
Your years require it, and 'tis necessary;
As necessary as meat to a young lady ;
Sleep cannot nourish more.

1 *Lady*. But might not all this be, and keep ye single ?
You take away variety in marriage, 19
Th' abundance of your pleasure you are barr'd then;
Is't not abundance that you aim at ?

Mar. Yes ; why was I made a woman ?

2 *Lady*. And ev'ry day a new ?

Mar. Why fair and young, but to use it ?

1 *Lady*. You're still i'th'right ; why would you marry then ?

Alt. Because a husband stops all doubts in this point,
And clears all passages.

2 *Lady*. What husband mean ye ?

Alt. A husband of an easy faith, a fool,
Made by her wealth, and moulded to her pleasure ;
One, though he sees himself become a monster,
Shall hold the door, and entertain the maker.

2 *Lady*. You grant there may be such a man.

1 *Lady.* Yes, marry; but how to bring him to this rare perfection.
2 *Lady.* They must be chosen so, things of no honour,
Nor outward honesty.
Mar. No, 'tis no matter;
I care not what they are, so they be comely.
2 *Lady.* Methinks now, a rich lawyer, some such fellow,
That carries credit, and a face of awe,
" But lies with nothing but his client's business."
Mar. No, there's no trusting them, they are too subtle;
The law has moulded them of natural mischief.
1 *Lady.* Then some grave governor,
Some man of honour, yet an easy man.
Mar. If he has honour, I'm undone; I'll none such.
Alt. With search, and wit, and labour,
I've found one out, a right one, and a perfect.
Mar. Is he a gentleman?
Alt. Yes, and a soldier; but as gentle as you'd wish him. A good fellow, and has good clothes, if he knew how to wear 'em.
Mar. Those I'll allow him;
They are for my credit. Does he understand
But little.
Alt. Very little?
Mar. 'Tis the better.
Have not the wars bred him up to anger?
Alt. No, he won't quarrel with a dog that bites him;

Let him be drunk or sober, he's one silence.
Mar. H'as no capacity what honour is;
For that's a soldier's good?
Alt. Honour's a thing too subtle for his wisdom;
If honour lie in eating, he's right honourable.
Mar. Is he so goodly a man, do you say?
Alt. As you shall see, lady;
But to all this he's but a trunk.
Mar. I'd have him so;
" I shall add branches to adorn him."
Go, find me out this man, and let me see him;
If he be that motion that you tell me of,
And make no more noise, I shall entertain him.
Let him be here.
Alt. He shall attend your ladyship. [*Exeunt.*

SCENE II.

A Street. Enter JUAN, ALONZO, *and* PEREZ.

Juan. Why, thou'rt not married indeed?
Per. No, no, pray think so.
Alas, I am a fellow of no reckoning!
Nor worth a lady's eye.
Alon. Wou'dst steal a fortune,
And make none of thy friends acquainted with it,
Nor bid us to thy wedding?
Per. No indeed.
There was no wisdom in't, to bid an artist,
An old seducer, to a female banquet.

I can cut up my pie without your instructions.
Juan. Was it the wench i'the veil?
Per. Basta, 'twas she.
The prettiest rogue that e'er you look'd upon;
The loving'st thief.
Juan. And is she rich withal too?
Per. A mine, a mine; there is no end of wealth,
Colonel.
I am an ass, a bashful fool. Pr'ythee, Colonel,
How do thy companies fill now?
Juan. You're merry, sir;
You intend a safer war at home, belike, now?
Per. I do not think I shall fight much this year,
Colonel;
I find myself given to my ease a little.
I care not if I sell my foolish company;
They're things of hazard.
Alon. How it angers me,
This fellow at first sight should win a lady,
A rich young wench——" And I, that have consum'd
" My time and art in searching out their subtleties,
" Like a fool'd alchymist, blow up my hopes still."
When shall we come to thy house, and be freely
merry?
Per. When I have manag'd her a little more.
I have an house to maintain an army.
Alon. If thy wife be fair, thou'lt have few less come
to thee.
Per. Where they'll get entertainment is the point;
Signior, I beat no drum.

" May be I'll march, after a month or two,
" To get a fresh stomach. I find, Colonel,
" A wantonness in wealth, methinks I agree not with.
" 'Tis such a trouble to be married too,
" And have a thousand things of great importance,
" Jewels and plate, and fooleries molest me,
" To have a man's brains whimsied with his wealth.
" Before I walked contentedly."

Enter Servant.

Ser. My mistress, sir, is sick, because you're absent.
She mourns, and will not eat.
Per. Alas, my jewel!
Come, I'll go with thee. Gentlemen, your fair leaves,
You see I'm ty'd a little to my yoke;
Pray, pardon me; would ye had both such loving wives. [*Exeunt* Perez *and Servant.*
Juan. I thank ye
For your old boots. Never be blank, Alonzo,
Because this fellow has out-stripp'd thy fortune.
" Tell me, ten days hence, what he is, and how
" The gracious state of matrimony stands with him."
Come, let's to dinner; when Margaritta comes,
We'll visit both; it may be then your fortune.
[*Exeunt.*

SCENE III.

A Chamber. Enter MARGARITTA, ALTEA, *and Ladies.*

Mar. Is he come ?
Alt. Yes, madam, he has been here this half hour.
I've question'd him of all that you can ask him,
And find him fit as you had made the man.
Mar. Call him in, Altea. [*Exit* Altea.

Enter LEON *and* ALTEA.

A man of a comely countenance. Pray ye come this way.
Is his mind so tame ?
Alt. Pray question him, and if you find him not
Fit for your purpose, shake him off, there's no harm done. 141
Mar. Can ye love a young lady ? How he blushes!
Alt. Leave twirling of your hat, and hold your head up.
And speak to th' lady.
Leon. Yes, I think I can ;
I must be taught ; I know not what it means, madam.
Mar. You shall be taught. And can you, when she pleases,
Go ride abroad, and stay a week or two ?
You shall have men and horses to attend ye,
And money in your purse.
Leon. Yes, I love riding ;
And when I am from home I am so merry.

Mar. Be as merry as you will. Can you as handsomely,
When you are sent for back, come with obedience,
And do your duty to the lady loves you?

Leon. Yes, sure, I shall.

Mar. And when you see her friends here,
Or, noble kinsmen, can you entertain
Their servants in the cellar, and be busied,
And hold your peace, whate'er you see or hear?

Leon. 'Twere fit I were hang'd else.

Mar. Come, salute me.

Leon. Ma'am!

Mar. How the fool shakes! I will not eat you, sir.
Can't you salute me?

Leon. Indeed I know not; but if your ladyship will please to instruct me, sure I shall learn.

Mar. Come on, then.

Leon. Come on, then. [*He kisses her.*

" *Mar.* Beshrew my heart, he kisses wondrous manly!
" Can you do any thing else?

" *Leon.* Indeed I know not; but if your Ladyship
" will please to instruct me, sure I shall learn."

Mar. You shall then be instructed.
If I should be this lady that affects ye;
Nay, say I marry ye?

Alt. Hark to the lady.

Mar. What money have ye?

Leon. None, madam, nor no friends.
I would do any thing to serve your ladyship.

Mar. You must not look to be my master, sir.
Nor talk i' the house as though you wore the breeches;
No, nor command in any thing.

Leon. I will not;
Alas, I am not able! I've no wit, madam.

Mar. Nor do not labour to arrive at any;
'Twill spoil your head. I take ye upon charity,
And like a servant ye must be unto me.
" As I behold your duty, I shall love you;
" And as you observe me, I may chance lie with ye."
Can you mark these?

Leon. Yes, indeed, forsooth.

Mar. There is one thing,
That if I take ye in, I put ye from me,
Utterly from me; you must not be saucy,
No, nor at any time familiar with me,
Scarce know me, when I call ye not.

Leon. I will not. Alas, I never knew myself sufficiently!

Mar. Nor must not now.

Leon. I'll be a dog to please ye.

Mar. Indeed you must fetch and carry as I appoint ye.

Leon. I were to blame else.

Mar. Kiss me again. [*Kisses her.*
" A strong fellow; there's vigour in his lips."
If you see me
Kiss any other, twenty in an hour, sir,
You must not start, nor be offended.

Leon. No, if you kiss a thousand, I shall be contented,

It will the better teach me how to please ye.
Alt. I told ye, madam.
Mar. 'Tis the man I wish'd for; the less you speak—
Leon. I'll never speak again, madam,
But when you charge me; then I'll speak softly too.
Mar. Get me a priest; I'll wed him instantly.
But when you're married, sir, you must wait on me,
And see ye observe my laws.
Leon, Else you shall hang me.
Mar. I'll give you better clothes when you deserve 'em.
Come in, and serve for witness.
Omnes. We shall, madam.
Mar. And then away to the city presently;
I'll to my new house, and new company.
Leon. A thousand crowns are thine; I'm a made man.
Alt. Do not break out too soon.
Leon. I know my time, wench. [*Exeunt.*

SCENE IV.

A grand Saloon. Enter CLARA *and* ESTIFANIA *with a Paper.*

Cla. What, have you caught him?
Estif. Yes.
Cla. And do you find him
A man of those hopes that you aim'd at?
Estif. Yes, too, and the most kind man;
" And the ablest, also,

" To give his wife content: he is sound as old wine,
" And to his soundness rises on the pallat;
" And there's the man."
I find him rich, too, Clara.

Cla. Hast thou married him?

Estif. What, dost thou think I fish without a bait, wench?
I bob for fools. He is mine own. I have him.
I told thee what would tickle him like a trout;
And as I cast it, so I caught him daintily;
And all he has I've 'stow'd at my devotion.

Cla. Does the lady know this? she's coming now to town:
Now, to live here, in this house.

Estif. Let her come,
She shall be welcome, I am prepar'd for her;
She's mad sure, if she be angry at my fortune;
For what I have made bold.

Cla. Dost thou not love him?

Estif. Yes, entirely well,
As long as there he stays and looks no farther
Into my ends; but when he doubts, I hate him;
And that wise hate will teach me how to cozen him;
" How to decline their wives, and curb their manners;
" To put a stern and strong rein to their natures:
" And holds he is an ass not worth acquaintance,
" That cannot mould a devil into obedience.
" I owe him a good turn for these opinions;
" And, as I find his temper, I may pay him."

Enter PEREZ.

O here he is; now you shall see a kind man.

Per. My Estifania, shall we to dinner, lamb?
I know thou stay'st for me.

Estif. I cannot eat else.

Per. I never enter, but methinks a paradise
Appears about me.

Estif. You're welcome to it, sir.

Per. I think I have the sweetest seat in Spain, wench.
Methinks the richest too. We'll eat i' the garden,
In one o' the arbours, there 'tis cool and pleasant;
And have our wine cool'd in the running fountain.
Who's that?

Estif. A friend of mine, sir.

Per. Of what breeding?

Estif. A gentlewoman, sir.

Per. What business has she?
Is she a woman learned i' the mathematics?
Can she tell fortunes?

Estif. More than I know, sir.

Per. Or has she e'er a letter from a kinswoman,
That must be deliver'd in my absence, wife?
Or comes she from the doctor to salute ye,
And learn your health? she looks not like a confessor.

Estif. What needs all this? why are you troubled, sir?
What do you suspect? she cannot cuckold ye:
She is a woman, sir, a very woman.

Per. Your very woman may do very well, sir,
Towards the matter; for though she cannot perform it

In her own person, she may do it by proxy.
Your rarest jugglers work still by conspiracy.

Estif. Cry ye mercy, husband, you are jealous then,
And haply suspect me.

Per. No, indeed, wife.

Estif. Methinks you should not till you have more cause,
And clearer too. I'm sure you've heard say, husband,
A woman forc'd will free herself through iron:
A happy, calm, and good wife discontented,
May be caught by tricks.

Per. No, no: I do but jest with ye.

Estif. To-morrow, friend, I'll see you.

Cla. I shall leave ye
Till then, and pray all may go sweetly with ye. [*Exit.*
[*Knocking.*

Estif. Why, where's the girl? who's at the door?
[*Knock.*

Per. Who knocks there?
Is't for the king you come, ye knock so boisterously?
Look to the door.

Enter Maid.

Maid. My lady, as I live, mistress, my lady's come;
She's at the door; I peep'd through, I saw her,
And a stately company of ladies with her.

Estif. This was a week too soon, but I must meet with her,
And set a new wheel going; and a subtle one
Must blind this mighty Mars, or I am ruin'd. [*Aside.*

Per. What, are they at the door?

Estif. Such, my Michael,
As you may bless the day they enter'd here;
Such for our good.

Per. 'Tis well.

Estif. Nay, 'twill be better
If you will let me but dispose the business,
And be a stranger to't, and not disturb me.
What have I now to do but advance your fortune?

Per. Do, I dare trust thee; I am asham'd I was angry.
I find thee a wise young wife.

Estif. I'll wise your worship
Before I leave ye. [*Aside.*] Pray ye walk by, and say nothing,
Only salute them, and leave the rest to me, sir;
I was born to make ye a man.

Per. The rogue speaks heartily;
Her good-will colours in her cheeks; I'm born to love her.
I must be gentle to these tender natures:
A soldier's rude harsh words befit not ladies;
Nor must we talk to them, as we talk to
Our officers. I'll give her way, for 'tis for me she
Works now; I am husband, heir, and all she has.

Enter MARGARITTA, LEON, ALTEA, *and* Ladies.

Who're these? I hate such flaunting things.
A woman of rare presence! excellent fair;
This is too big, sure, for a bawdy-house;
Too open seated too.

Estif. My husband, lady.

Mar. You've gain'd a proper man.

Per. Whate'er I am, I am your servant, lady. [*Kisses.*

Estif. Sir, be rul'd now, [*Apart to* Perez.
And I shall make you rich: this is my cousin;
That gentleman doats on her, even to death.
See how he observes her.

Per. She is a goodly woman.

Estif. She is a mirror.
But she is poor, she were for a prince's side else.
This house she has brought him to as to her own,
And presuming upon me, and on my courtesy——
Conceive me short; he knows not but she's wealthy:
" Or if he did know otherwise, 'twere all one,
" He's so far gone."

Per. Forward; she's a rare face.

Estif. This we must carry with discretion, husband,
And yield unto her for four days.

Per. Yield our house up, our goods and wealth!

Estif. All this is but seeming.—Do you see this writing?
Two hundred pounds a year, when they are married,
Has she seal'd to for our good—The time is unfit now;
I'll shew it you to-morrow.

Per. All the house?

Estif. All, all; and we'll remove, too, to confirm him.
They'll into the country suddenly again,
" After they're match'd, and then she'll open to him."

Per. The whole possession, wife? Look what you do.
A part o' the house.

Estif. No, no, they shall have all,
And take their pleasure too; 'tis for our 'vantage.
Why, what's four days? Had you a sister, sir,
A niece, or mistress, that requir'd this courtesy,
And should I make a scruple to do you good?

Per. If easily it would come back.

Estif. I swear, sir, as easily as it came on.
" Is't not pity
" To let such a gentlewoman for a little help——"
You give away no house.

Per. Clear but that question.

Estif. I'll put the writings into your hand.

Per. Well then.

Estif. And you shall keep them safe.

Per. I'm satisfied.—Would I had the wench too.

Estif. When she has married him,
So infinite his love is link'd unto her,
You, I, or any one that helps at this pinch,
May have Heav'n knows what.

Per. I'll remove my trunks straight,
And take some poor house by, 'tis but for four days.

Estif. I have a poor old friend; there we will be.

Per. 'Tis well then.

Estif. Go handsome off, and leave the house clear.

Per. Well.

Estif. That little stuff we'll use shall follow after;
And a boy to guide ye. Peace, and we are made both.

Mar. Come, let's go in. Are all the rooms kept sweet, wench?

Estif. They're sweet and neat. [*Exit* Perez.

Mar. Why, where's your husband?
Estif. Gone, madam.
When you come to your own, he must give place, lady.
Mar. Well, send you joy, you would not let me know't,
Yet I shall not forget ye.
Estif. Thank your ladyship.
" *Mar.* Come, lead me." [*Exeunt.*

ACT III. SCENE I.

A Chamber. Enter MARGARITTA *and* ALTEA.

ALTEA.

ARE you at ease now? Is your heart at rest,
" Now you have got a shadow, an umbrella,
" To keep the scorching world's opinion
" From your fair credit?"
Mar. I am at peace, Altea.
If he continue but the same he shews,
And be a master of that ignorance
He outwardly professes, I am happy.
" The pleasure I shall live in, and the freedom
" Without the squint eye of the law upon me,
" Or prating liberty of tongues that envy!"
Alt. You're a made woman.
Mar. But if he should prove now
A crafty and dissembling kind of husband,

One read in knavery, and brought up in the art
Of villainy conceal'd.

Alt. My life, an innocent.

Mar. That's it I aim at.
That's it I hope too, then I'm sure I rule him:
" For innocents are like obedient children,
" Brought up under a hard mother-in-law, a cruel,
" Who, being not us'd to breakfasts and collations,
" When they have coarse bread offered, are thankful,
" And take it for a favour too."
Are the rooms made ready
To entertain my friends? I long to dance now,
" And to be wanton. Let me have a song. Is the great couch up
" The duke of Medina sent?

" *Alt.* 'Tis up and ready.

" *Mar.* And day-beds in all chambers?

Alt. " In all, lady."
Your house is nothing now but various pleasures.
The gallants begin to gaze too.

Mar. Let 'em gaze on.
I was brought up a courtier, high and happy;
And company is my delight and courtship;
And handsome servants at my will. Where's my good husband?
Where does he wait?

Alt. He knows his distance, madam.
I warrant ye he is busy in the cellar
Among his fellow-servants, or asleep,
Till your commands awake him.

Enter LEON *and* LORENZO.

Mar. 'Tis well, Altea,
It should be so; my ward I must preserve him.
Who sent for him? How dare he come uncall'd for?
His bonnet on too!

Alt. Sure he sees you not.

Mar. How scornfully he looks!

Leon. Are all the chambers
Deck'd and adorn'd thus for my lady's pleasure?
New hangings every hour for entertainment?
And new plate bought, new jewels to give lustre?

Ser. They are, and yet there must be more and richer;
It is her will.

Leon. Hum, is it so? 'Tis excellent.
Is it her will, too, to have feasts and banquets,
Revels and masques?

Ser. She ever lov'd 'em dearly;
And we shall have the bravest house kept now, sir.
I must not call ye master; she has warn'd me;
Nor must not put my hat off to you.

Leon. 'Tis no fashion.
What though I be her husband, I'm your fellow;
I may cut first?

Ser. That's as you shall deserve, sir.

Leon. I thank you, sir.—" And when I lie with her—

" *Ser.* May be I'll light ye:
" On the same point you may do me that service."

Enter a Lady.

1 *Lady.* Madam, the Duke Medina, with some captains,

Will come to dinner, and have sent rare wine,
And their best services.
Mar. They shall be welcome.
See all be ready in the noblest fashion;
" The house perfum'd.
" Now I shall take my pleasure,
" And not my neighbour justice maunder at me."
Go, get your best clothes on; but till I call ye,
Be sure you be not seen. Dine with the gentlewomen,
And behave yourself handsomely, sir, 'tis for my credit.

Enter a second Lady.

2 *Lady.* Madam, the lady Julia——
Leon. That's a bawd;
A three-pil'd bawd; bawd major to the army.
2 *Lady.* Has brought her coach to wait upon your ladyship,
And to be inform'd if you will take the air this morning.
Leon. The neat air of her nunnery.
Mar. Tell her no; i' the afternoon I'll call on her.
2 *Lady.* I will, madam. [*Exit.*
" *Mar.* Why are you not gone to prepare yourself?
" May be you shall be sewer to the first course.
" A portly presence. Altea, he looks lean—
" 'Tis a vast knave, he will not keep his flesh well.
" *Alt.* A willing, madam, one that needs no spurring."
Leon. Faith, madam, in my little understanding,
You'd better entertain your honest neighbours,

Your friends about ye, that may speak well of ye,
And give a worthy mention of your bounty.

Mar. How now, what this?

Leon. 'Tis only to persuade ye
Courtiers are tickle things to deal withal,
A kind of march-pane men that will not last, madam
An egg and pepper goes farther than their potions;
And in a well-knit body, a poor parsnip 108
Will play his prize above their strong potables.

Mar. The fellow's mad!

Leon. He that shall counsel ladies,
That hath both liquorish and ambitious eyes,
Is either mad or drunk, let him speak gospel.

Alt. He breaks out modestly.

Leon. Pray ye be not angry;
My indiscretion has made bold to tell ye
What you'll find true.

Mar. Thou dar'st not talk?

Leon. Not much, madam;
You have a tie upon your servant's tongue,
He dare not be so bold as reason bids him;
'Twere fit there were a stronger on your temper.
Ne'er look so stern upon me, I'm your husband:
But what are husbands? Read the New World's Wonders,
Such husbands as this monstrous world produces,
And you will scarce find such strange deformities;
They're shadows to conceal your venal virtues; 121
Sails to your mills, that grind with all occasions;
Balls that lie by you, to wash out your stains;

And bills nail'd up with horns before your doors,
To rent out wantonness.

Mar. Do you hear him talk?

Leon. I've done, madam:
An ox once spoke, as learned men deliver;
Shortly I shall be such, then I'll speak wonders.
'Till when I tie myself to my obedience. [*Exit.*

Mar. First I'll untie myself. Did you mark the gentleman,
How boldly and how saucily he talk'd,
And how unlike the lump I took him for!
" The piece of ignorant dough, he stood up to me,
" And rated my commands."
This was your providence,
Your wisdom, to elect this gentleman,
Your excellent forecast in the man, your knowledge;
What think ye now?

Alt. I think him an ass still.
This boldness some of your people have blown into him,
This wisdom too, with strong wine; 'tis a tyrant,
And a philosopher also, and finds out reasons.

Mar. I'll have my cellar lock'd, no school kept there,
Nor no discovery. I'll turn my drunkards,
Such as are understanding in their draughts,
And dispute learnedly the whys and wherefores,
To grass immediately: I'll keep all fools,
Sober or drunk, still fools that shall know nothing.
Nothing belongs to mankind but obedience,

And such a hand I'll keep over this husband.
Alt. He'll fall again: my life, he cries by this time:
Keep him from drink, he's a high constitution.

Enter LEON.

Leon. Shall I wear my new suit, madam?
Mar. No, your old clothes.
And get you into the country presently,
And see my hawks well train'd: you shall have victuals,
Such as are fit for saucy palates, sir,
And lodgings with the hinds, it is too good too.
Leon. Good madam, be not so rough with repentance.
Alt. You see how he's come round again.
Mar. I see not what I expect to see.
Leon. You shall see, madam, if it please your ladyship.
Alt. He's humbled;
Forgive, good lady.
Mar. Well, go get you handsome,
And let me hear no more.
Leon. Have ye yet no feeling?
I'll pinch you to the bones then, my proud lady. [*Exit.*
Mar. See you preserve him thus, upon my favour.
You know his temper, tie him to the grindstone;
The next rebellion I'll be rid of him.
I'll have no needy rascals I tie to me
Dispute my life. Come in, and see all handsome.
Alt. I hope to see you so too, I've wrought ill else.
[*Exeunt.*

SCENE II.

An ordinary Apartment. *Enter* PEREZ.

Per. Shall I
Never return to mine own house again?
We're lodg'd here in the miserablest dog-hole,
A conjuror's circle gives content above it;
A hawk's mew is a princely palace to it:
We have a bed no bigger than a basket,
And we lie like butter clapt together,
And sweat ourselves to sauce immediately;
The fumes are infinite inhabit here too,
" And to that so thick they cut like marmalade;"
So various too, they'll pose a gold finder.
Never return to mine own paradise——
Why, wife, I say; why, Estifania?
Estif. [*within.*] I'm going presently.
Per. Make haste, good jewel.
I'm like the people that live in the sweet islands:
I die, I die, if I stay but one day more here.
" My lungs are rotten with the damps that rise,
" And I cough nothing now but stinks of all sorts."
The inhabitants we have are two starv'd rats,
For they're not able to maintain a cat here,
And those appear as fearful as two devils;
They've eat a map o' the whole world up already,
And if we stay a night, we're gone for company.
There's an old woman that's now grown to marble,
Dry'd in this brick-kiln, and she sits i'the chimney,

(Which is but three tiles rais'd, like a house of cards)
The true proportion of an old smoak'd Sybil.
There is a young thing too, that nature meant
For a maid servant, but 'tis now a monster;
She has a husk about her like a chesnut,
With laziness, and living under the line here;
And these two make a hollow sound together,
Like frogs, or winds between two doors that murmur.

Enter ESTIFANIA.

Mercy deliver me. Oh, are you come, wife;
Shall we be free again?
Estif. I am now going,
And you shall presently to your own house, sir:
The remembrance of this small vexation
Will be argument of mirth for ever.
By that time you have said your orisons,
And broke your fast, I shall be back, and ready
To usher you to your old content, your freedom.
Per. Break my fast, break my neck rather.
Is there any thing here to eat
But one another, like a race of cannibals?
A piece of butter'd wall you think is excellent.
Let's have our house again immediately,
And pray ye take heed unto the furniture,
None be embezzled.
Estif. Not a pin, I warrant ye.
Per. And let 'em instantly depart.
Estif. They shall both; there's reason in all courtesy;
For by this time I know she has acquainted him,

And has provided too: she sent me word, sir,
And will give over gratefully unto you.
Per. I will walk i'the church-yard;
The dead cannot offend more than these living.
An hour hence I'll expect ye.
Estif. I'll not fail, sir.
Per. And do you hear? let's have a handsome dinner,
And see all things be decent as they have been;
And let me have a strong bath to restore me;
I stink like a stale-fish shambles, or an oil-shop.
Estif. You shall have all, which some interpret nothing.
I'll send ye people for the trunks afore-hand,
" And for the stuff."
Per. Let 'em be known and honest;
And do my service to your niece.
Estif. I shall, sir:
But if I come not at my hour, come thither,
That they may give you thanks for your fair courtesy,
And pray you, be brave for my sake.
Per. I observe ye. [*Exeunt.*

SCENE III.

A Street. Enter JUAN DE CASTRO, SANCHO, *and* CACAFOGO.

San. Thou'rt very brave.
Caca. I've reason, I have money.
San. Is money reason?

Caca. Yes, and rhyme too, Captain.
If you've no money, you're an ass.
San. I thank ye.
Caca. Ye've manners, ever thank him that has money.
San. Wilt thou lend me any?
Caca. Not a farthing, Captain:
Captains are casual things.
San. Why so are all men. Thou sha't have my bond.
Caca. Nor bonds nor fetters, Captain.
My money is my own, I make no doubt on't.
Juan, What dost thou do with it?
Caca. Put it to pious uses.
Buy wine and wenches, and undo young coxcombs
That would undo me.
Juan. Are those hospitals?
Caca. I first provide to fill my hospitals
With creatures of mine own, that I know wretched,
And then I build: those are more bound to pray for me:
Besides, I keep th' inheritance in my name still.
Juan. A provident charity. Are you for the wars, sir?
Caca. I am not poor enough to be a soldier,
Nor have I faith enough to ward a bullet;
This is no lining for a trench, I take it.
Juan. Ye have said wisely.
Caca. Had you but my money,
You'd swear it, Colonel. I had rather drill at home
A hundred thousand crowns, and with more honour,
Than exercise ten thousand fools with nothing.
A wise man safely feeds, fools cut their fingers.
San. A right state usurer. Why dost not marry,
And live a reverend justice?

Caca. Is it not nobler to command a reverend justice than to be one?
And for a wife, what need I marry, Captain,
When every courteous fool that owes me money,
Owes me his wife too, to appease my fury?

Juan. Wilt thou go to dinner with us?

Caca. I will go, and view the pearl of Spain, the orient
Fair one, the rich one too; and I will be respected.
I bear my patent here; I will talk to her;
And when your captainships shall stand aloof,
And pick your noses, I will pick the purse
Of her affection.

Juan. The Duke dines there to-day too, the Duke of Medina.

Caca. Let the king dine there,
He owes me money, and so far's my creature,
And certainly I may make bold with mine own, Captain.

San. Thou wilt eat monstrously.

Caca. Like a true born Spaniard:
Eat as I were in England, where the beef grows:
And I will drink abundantly, and then
Talk ye as wantonly as Ovid did,
To stir the intellectuals of the ladies;
I learnt it of my father's amorous scrivener.

Juan. If we should play now, you must supply me.

Caca. You must pawn a horse troop,
And then have at ye, Colonel.

San. Come, let's go.
This rascal will make rare sport. How the ladies
Will laugh at him!

Juan. If I light on him I'll make his purse sweat too.
Caca. Will ye lead, gentlemen? [*Exeunt.*

SCENE IV.

An ordinary Apartment. Enter PEREZ, *Old Woman, and Maid.*

Per. Nay, pray ye come out, and let me understand ye,
And tune your pipe a little higher, lady;
I'll hold ye fast. How came my trunks open?
And my goods gone? What pick-lock spirit——
Old Wom. Ha! What would ye have?
Per. My goods again. How came my trunks all open?
Old Wom. Are your trunks all open?
Per. Yes, and cloaths gone,
And chains and jewels. How she smells like hung beef!
The palsy, and pick-locks. Fye, how she belches
The spirit of garlick!
Old Wom. Where's your gentlewoman?
The young fair woman?
Per. What's that to my question?
She is my wife, and gone about my business.
Maid. Is she your wife, sir?
Per. Yes, sir: is that a wonder?
Is the name of wife unknown here?
Old Wom. Is she duly and truly your wife?
Per. Duly and truly my wife! I think so,
For I married her. It was no vision sure!

Maid. She has the keys, sir.

Per. I know she has; but who has all my goods, spirit?

Old Wom. If you be married to that gentlewoman,
You are a wretched man: she has twenty husbands.

Maid. She tells you true.

Old Wom. And she has cozen'd all, sir.

Per. The devil she has! I had a fair house with her,
That stands hard by, and furnish'd royally.

Old Wom. You're cozen'd too, 'tis none of her's, good gentleman,
It is a lady's.

Maid. The lady Margaritta; she was her servant,
And kept the house; but going from her, sir,
For some lewd tricks she play'd.

Per. Plague o' the devil;
Am I, i'the full meridian of my wisdom,
Cheated by a stale quean! What kind of lady
Is that that owns the house?

Old Wom. A young sweet lady.

Per. Of low stature.

Old Wom. She's indeed but little, but she's wondrous fair.

Per. I feel I'm cozen'd:
Now I am sensible I am undone.
This is the very woman sure, that cousin,
She told me would entreat but for four days
To make the house hers—I am entreated sweetly.

Maid. When she went out this morning, I saw, sir,
She had two women at the door attending,

And there she gave 'em things, and loaded 'em:
But what they were——I heard your trunks too open,
If they be yours.

Per. They were mine while they were laden;
But now they've cast their calves, they're not worth owning.
Was she her mistress, say you?

Old Wom. Her own mistress, her very mistress, sir; and all you saw
About and in that house was hers.

Per. No plate, no jewels, nor no hangings?

Maid. Not a farthing; she's poor, sir, a poor shifting thing.

Per. No money?

Old Wom. Abominable poor, as poor as we are,
Money as rare to her, unless she steal it.
But for one single gown her lady gave her,
She might go bare, good gentlewoman.

Per. I'm mad now:
I think I am as poor as she, I'm wild else.
One single suit I have left too, and that's all,
And if she steals that she must flay me for it.
Where does she use?

Old Wom. You may find the truth as soon.
Alas, a thousand conceal'd corners, sir, she lurks in;
And here she gets a fleece, and there another,
And lives in mists and smokes where none can find her.

Per. Is she a whore too?

Old Wom. Little better, gentleman:
I dare not say she is so, sir, because

She's yours, sir: these five years she has firk'd
A pretty living. "Until she came to serve.
"I fear he will knock my brains out for lying."
Per. She has firk'd me finely.
A whore and thief; two excellent moral learnings
In one she saint. I hope to see her legend.
Have I been fear'd for my discoveries,
And been courted by all women to conceal 'em;
Have I so long studied the art of this sex,
And read the warning to young gentlemen;
Have I profess'd to tame the pride of ladies,
And make them bear all tests; and am I trick'd now?
Caught in my own noose? Here's a rial left yet,
There's for your lodging, and your meat for a week;
A silk-worm lives at a more plentiful ordinary,
And sleeps in a sweeter box,
Farewell, great grandmother,
If I do find you were an accessary,
'Tis but the cutting off two smoaking minutes!
I'll hang ye presently.
Old Wom. And I deserve it—I tell you truth.
Per. Not I, I am an ass, mother.
Old Wom. *O the rogue, the villain! Is this usage for the fair sex.* [*Exeunt.*

SCENE V.

A grand Apartment. Enter the Duke of MEDINA, JUAN DE CASTRO, ALONZO, SANCHO, CACAFOGO, *and Attendants.*

Duke. A goodly house.
Juan. And richly furnish'd too, sir.
Alon. Hung wantonly; I like that preparation;
It stirs the blood unto a hopeful banquet,
And intimates the mistress free and jovial;
I love a house where pleasure prepares welcome.
Duke. Now, Cacafogo, how like you this mansion?
'Twere a brave pawn.
Caca. I shall be master of it;
'Twas built for my bulk, the rooms are wide and spacious,
Airy and full of ease, and that I love well.
I'll tell you when I taste the wine, my lord;
And take the height of her table with my stomach,
How my affection stands to the young lady.

Enter MARGARITTA, ALTEA, *Ladies, and Servant.*

Mar. All welcome to your Grace, and to these soldiers,
You honour my poor house with your fair presence;
Those few slight pleasures that inhabit here, sir,
I do beseech your Grace command, they're yours,
Your servant but preserves 'em to delight ye.
Duke. I thank ye lady, I am bold to visit ye,
Once more to bless mine eyes with your sweet beauty,

'T has been a long night since you left the court,
For till I saw you now, no day broke to me.

Mar. Bring in the Duke's meat.

San. She's most excellent.

Juan. Most admirable fair as e'er I look'd on;
I rather would command her than my regiment.

Caca. I'll have a fling, 'tis but a thousand ducats,
Which I can cozen up in ten days.
" And some few jewels to justify my knavery.
" Say, shall I marry her, she'll get more money
" Than all my usury put my knavery to it;
" She appears the most infallible way of purchase.
" I could wish her a size or two stronger for the encounter,
" For I am like a lion where I lay hold:
" But these lambs will endure a plaguy load
" And never bleat neither; that, sir, time has taught us.
" I am so virtuous now I cannot speak to her,
" The errantest shame-fac'd ass; I broil away too."

Enter LEON.

Mar. Why, where's this dinner?

Leon. 'Tis not ready, madam,
Nor shall it be, until I know the guests too,
Nor are they fairly welcome till I bid 'em.

Juan. Is not this my Alferes? he looks another thing;
Are miracles a foot again?

Mar. Why, sirrah; why, sirrah, you!

Leon. I hear you, saucy woman;
And as you are my wife, command your absence,

And know your duty; 'tis the crown of modesty.

Duke. Your wife!

Leon. Yes, good my lord, I am her husband,
And, pray take notice, that I claim that honour,
And will maintain it.

Caca. If thou be'st her husband,
I am determin'd thou shalt be my cuckold;
I'll be thy faithful friend.

Leon. Peace, dirt and dunghill,
I will not lose my anger on a rascal.
Provoke me more, I'll beat thy blown-up body
Till thou rebound'st again like a tennis-ball.

Caca. I'll talk with you another time. [*Exit.*

Alon. This is miraculous!

San. Is this the fellow
That had the patience to become a fool,
" A flutter'd fool, and on a sudden break,
" As if he would shew a wonder to the world,
" Both in bravery and fortune too?"
I am astonish'd!

Mar. I'll be divorc'd immediately.

Leon. You shall not.
You shall not have so much will to be wicked.
I am more tender of your honour, lady.
You took me for a shadow,
You took me to gloss over your discredit,
To be your fool,
You had thought you had found a coxcomb,
I'm innocent of any foul dishonour I mean to ye.
Only I will be known to be your lord now,

And be a fair one too, or I will fall for't.
Mar. I do command ye from me, thou poor fellow,
Thou cozen'd fool.
Leon. Thou cozen'd fool,
I will not be commanded: I'm above ye.
You may divorce me from your favour, lady,
But from your 'state you never shall. I'll hold that,
And hold it to my use, the law allows it.
And then maintain your wantonness, I'll wink at it.
Mar. Am I brav'd thus in mine own house?
Leon. 'Tis mine, madam,
You are deceiv'd, I'm lord of it, I rule it,
And all that's in't; you've nothing to do here, madam,
But as a servant to sweep clean the lodgings,
And at my farther will to do me service,
And so I'll keep it.
Mar. 'Tis well.
Leon. It shall be better.
Mar. As you love me, give way.
Leon. I will give none, madam;
I stand upon the ground of my own honour,
And will maintain it; you shall know me now
To be an understanding, feeling man,
And sensible of what a woman aims at;
A young proud woman, that has will to sail with;
A wanton woman, that her blood provokes too.
I cast my cloud off, and appear myself,
The master of this little piece of mischief,
And I will put a spell about your feet, lady;
They shall not wander but where I give way now.

Duke. Is this the fellow that the people pointed at,
For the mere sign of man, the walking image?
He speaks wond'rous highly.
Leon. As a husband ought, sir,
In his own house, and it becomes me well too.
I think your grace would grieve if you were put to it,
To have a wife or servant of your own,
(For wives are reckon'd in the rank of servants)
Under your own roof to command ye.
" *Juan.* Brave! a strange conversion; thou shalt lead
" In chief now."
Duke. Is there no difference betwixt her and you, sir?
Leon. Not now my lord, my fortune makes me ev'n,
And, as I am an honest man, I'm nobler.
Mar. Get me my coach.
Leon. Let me see who dares get it
Till I command; I'll make him draw your coach
And eat your coach too (which will be hard diet)
That executes your will; or, take your coach, lady,
I give you liberty; and take your people
Which I turn off; and take your will abroad with ye,
Take all these freely, but take me no more,
And so farewell.
Duke. Nay, sir, you shall not carry it
So bravely off; you shall not wrong a lady
In a high huffing strain, and think to bear it.
We shall not stand by as bawds to your brave fury.
To see a lady weep—*Draw, sir.*
Leon. They're tears of anger,

Wrung from her rage, because her will prevails not.
She would e'en now swoon if she could not cry,
" Else they were excellent, and I should grieve too ;
" But falling thus, they shew nor sweet nor orient."
Put up my lord, this is oppression,
And calls the sword of justice to relieve me,
The law to lend her hand, the king to right me,
All which shall understand how you provoke me.
In mine own house to brave me, is this princely?
Then to my guard, and if I spare your grace,
And do not make this place your monument,
Too rich a tomb for such a rude behaviour,
Mercy forsake me. [*Draws.*
I have a cause will kill a thousand of ye. 561

Juan. Hold, fair sir, I beseech ye,
The gentleman but pleads his own right nobly.

Leon. He that dares strike against the husband's freedom,
The husband's curse stick to him, a tam'd cuckold,
His wife be fair and young, but most dishonest,
Most impudent, and he have no feeling of it,
" No conscience to reclaim her from a monster ;"
Let her lie by him like a flattering ruin,
And at one instant kill both name and honour :
" Let him be lost, no eye to weep his end,
" Nor find no earth that's base enough to bury him."
Now, sir, fall on, I'm ready to oppose ye.

Duke. I've better thought. I pray, sir, use your wife well.

Leon. Mine own humanity will teach me that, sir.

And now, you're welcome all, and we'll to dinner;
This is my wedding-day.

Duke. I'll cross your joy yet.

Juan. I've seen a miracle, hold thine own, soldier.
Sure they dare fight in fire that conquer women.

" *San.* He has beaten all my loose thoughts out of me,
" As if he had thresh'd 'em out of the husk."

Enter PEREZ.

Per. 'Save ye, which is the lady of the house?

Leon. That's she, sir, that good-natur'd pretty lady,
If you'd speak with her.

Juan. Don Michael!

Per. Pray do not know me, I am full of business.
When I have more time I'll be merry with ye.
It is the woman. Good madam, tell me truly,
Had you a maid call'd Estifania!

Mar. Yes, truly had I.

Per. Was she a maid d'you think?

Mar. I dare not swear for her.———
For she had but a scant fame.

Per. Was she your kinswoman?

Mar. Not that I ever knew; now I look better,
I think you married her, give you much joy, sir.

Per. Give me a halter.

Mar. You may reclaim her; 'twas a wild young girl.

Per. Is not this house mine, madam?
Was not she owner of it? " Pray, speak truly."

Mar. No, certainly, I'm sure my money paid for it,
And ne'er remember yet I gave it you, sir.

Per. The hangings and the plate too?
Mar. All are mine, sir,
And every thing you see about the building;
She only kept my house when I was absent;
And so I'll keep it, I was weary of her.
Per. Where is your maid?
Mar. Do you not know that have her?
She's yours now, why should I look after her?
Since that first hour I came I never saw her.
Per. I saw her later, would the devil had had her.
It is all true, I find; a wild-fire take her.
Juan. Is thy wife with child, Don Michael? Thy excellent wife.
Art thou a man yet?
Alon, When shall we come and visit thee?
San. And eat some rare fruit? Thou hast admirable orchards.
You are so jealous now! Pox o' your jealousy,
How scornfully you look.
Per. Pr'ythee leave fooling,
I'm in no humour now to fool and prattle.
Did she ne'er play the wag with you?
Mar. Yes, many times,
So often that I was asham'd to keep her.
But I forgave her, sir, in hopes she'd mend still;
And had not you o' the instant married her,
I'd put her off.
Per. I thank ye; I am blest still;
Which way so'er I turn I'm a made man.
Miserably gull'd beyond recovery.

Juan. You'll stay and dine?

Per. Certain I cannot, captain.
Hark in thine ear, I am the arrant'st puppy,
The miserablest ass!—But I must leave ye.
I am in haste, in haste. Bless you, good madam,
And may you prove as good as my wife.

Leon. *What then, sir?*

Per. *No matter, if the devil had one to fetch the other.*

[*Exit* Perez.

Leon. Will you walk in, sir, will your grace but honour me,
And taste our dinner? You are nobly welcome,
All anger's past, I hope, and I shall serve ye. [*Exeunt.*

Act IV. SCENE I.

A Street. Enter PEREZ.

Perez.

I'LL to a conjurer, but I'll find this pole-cat,
This pilfering whore. A plague of veils, I cry,
And covers for the impudence of women,
Their sanctity in show will deceive devils.
It is my evil angel, let me bless me.

Enter ESTIFANIA, *with a casket.*

Estif. 'Tis he! I'm caught. I must stand to it stoutly,
And show no shake of fear. I see he's angry,
Vex'd at the uttermost.

Per. My worthy wife,
I have been looking of your modesty
All the town over.
Estif. My most noble husband,
I'm glad I have found ye; for in truth I'm weary,
Weary and lame with looking out your lordship.
Per. I've been in bawdy houses——
Estif. I believe you, and very lately too.
Per. 'Pray ye, pardon me;
To seek your ladyship, I have been in cellars,
In private cellars, where the thirsty bawds
Hear your confessions; I have been at plays,
To look you out among the youthful actors;
At puppet-shows, you are mistress of the motions;
" At gossiping I hearken'd after you,
" But among those confusions of lewd tongues,
" There's no distinguishing beyond a Babel;
" I was amongst the nuns, because you sing well,
" But they say yours are bawdy songs, and they mourn for ye;"
And last, I went to church to seek you out,
'Tis so long since you were there, they have forgot you.
Estif. You've had a pretty progress; I'll tell mine now.
To look you out, I went to twenty taverns——
Per. And are you sober?
Estif. Yes, I reel not yet, sir;
Where I saw twenty drunk, most of 'em soldiers,
There I had great hope to find you disguis'd too;
From hence to the dicing-house, there I found quarrels

Needless and fenceless, swords, pots, and candlesticks,
Tables, and stools; and all in one confusion,
And no man knew his friend. I left this chaos,
And to the surgeon's went, he will'd me stay,
For, says he, learnedly, if he be tippled,
Twenty to one he whores, and then I hear of him;
If he be mad, he quarrels, then he comes too.
I sought ye where no safe thing would have ventur'd,
Amongst diseases, base and vile, vile women,
For I remember'd your old Roman axiom,
The more the danger, still the more the honour.
Last, to your confessor I came, who told me,
You were too proud to pray? and here I've found ye.

Per. She bears up bravely, and the rogue is witty,
But I shall dash it instantly to nothing.
Here leave we off our wanton languages,
And now conclude we in a sharper tongue.
Why am I cozen'd?——

Estif. Why am I abus'd?

Per. Thou most vile, base, abominable——

Estif. Captain.

Per. Thou stinking, over-stew'd, incorrigible——

Estif. Captain.

Per. Do you echo me?

Estif. Yes, sir, and go before ye,
And round about ye, why do you rail at me,
For that was your own sin, your own knavery.

Per. And brave me too?

Estif. You'd best now draw your sword, captain!
Draw it upon a woman, do, brave captain,

Upon your wife, Oh, most renown'd captain!
Per. A plague upon thee, answer me directly;
Why didst thou marry me?
Estif. To be my husband;
I thought you had had infinite, but I'm cozen'd.
Per. Why didst thou flatter me, and shew me wonders?
A house and riches, when they are but shadows.
Shadows to me!
Estif. Why did you work on me?
It was but my part to requite you, sir,
With your strong soldier's wit, and swore you'd bring me
So much in chains, so much in jewels, husband,
So much in right rich clothes?
Per. Thou hast 'em rascal;
I gave 'em to thy hands, my trunks and all,
And thou hast open'd them, and sold my treasure.
Estif. Sir, there's your treasure, sell it to a tinker
To mend old kettles! Is this noble usage?
Let all the world view here the captain's treasure.
A man would think now these were worthy matters;
Here's a shoeing-horn chain gilt over, how it scenteth,
Worse than the dirty mouldy heels it serv'd for;
And here's another of a lesser value,
So little I would shame to tie my dog in't,
These are my jointure; blush and save a labour,
Or these else will blush for ye.
Per. A fire subtile ye, are ye so crafty?
Estif. Here's a goodly jewel,

Did not you win this at Goletta, captain?
Or took it in the field from some brave bashaw?
See how it sparkles——Like an old lady's eyes;
" And fills each room with light like a close lanthorn,
This would do rarely in an abbey window,
" To cozen pilgrims."

Per. Pr'ythee leave prating.

Estif. And here's a chain of whitings eyes for pearls,
A mussel-monger would have made a better.

Per. Nay, pr'ythee wife, my clothes, my clothes.

Estif. I'll tell ye,
Your clothes are parallels to these, all counterfeit.
Put these and them on, you're a man of copper,
" A kind of candlestick,"
A copper, a copper captain; these you thought, my husband,
To have cozen'd me withal, but I am quit with you.

Per. Is there no house then, nor no grounds about it?
No plate nor hangings?

Estif. There are none, sweet husband.
Shadow for shadow is as equal justice.

[*Perez sings—Estif sings.*

Can you rail now? Pray put your fury up, sir,
And speak great words, you are a soldier, thunder.

Per. I will speak little, I have play'd the fool,
And so I am rewarded.

Estif. You have spoke well, sir;
And now I see you're so conformable,
I'll heighten you again. Go to your house,
They're packing to be gone, you must sup there,

I'll meet you, and bring clothes and clean linen after,
And all things shall be well. I'll colt you once more,
And teach you to bring copper.

Per. Tell me one thing,
I do beseech thee tell me truth, wife;
However, I forgive thee; art thou honest?
The beldam swore——

Estif. I bid her tell you so, sir,
It was my plot; alas, my credulous husband;
The lady told you too———

Per. Most strange things of thee.

Estif. Still 'twas my way, and all to try your suff'rance.
And she denied the house?

Per. She knew me not,
No, nor title that I had,

Estif. 'Twas well carried;
No more, I'm right and straight.

Per. I would believe thee,
But, Heaven knows, how my heart is; will ye follow me?

Estif. I'll be there straight.

Per. I'm fool'd, yet dare not find it. [*Exit Perez.*

Estif. Go, silly fool? thou may'st be a good soldier
In open fields, but for our private service
Thou art an ass. "I'll make thee so, or miss else."

Enter CACAFOGO.

Here comes another trout that I must tickle,
And tickle daintily, I've lost my end else.
May I crave your leave, sir?

Caca. Pr'ythee be answer'd, thou shalt crave no leave,

I'm in my meditations, do not vex me,
A beaten thing, but this hour a most bruis'd thing,
That people had compassion on, "it look'd so:
"The next Sir Palmerin. Here's fine proportion!
"An ass, and then an elephant. Sweet justice!
"There's no way left to come at her now, no craving,
"If money could come near, yet I would pay him;"
I have a mind to make him a huge cuckold,
And money may do much; a thousand ducats!
'Tis but the letting blood of a rank heir.

Estif. 'Pray you, hear me.

Caca. I know thou hast some wedding-ring to pawn now,
Of silver gilt, with a blind posy in't:
"Love and a mill-horse should go round together:"
Or thy child's whistle, or thy squirrel's chain.
I'll none of 'em. I would she did but know me.
Or would this fellow had but use of money,
That I might come in any way.

Estif. I'm gone, sir;
And I shall tell the beauty sent me to ye;
The lady Margaritta——

Caca. Stay, I pr'ythee.
What is thy will? I turn me wholly to ye;
And talk now till thy tongue ake, I will hear ye.

Estif. She would entreat you, sir.

Caca. She shall command, sir;
Let it be so; I beseech thee, my sweet gentlewoman,
Do not forget thyself.

Estif. She does command then

This courtesy, because she knows you're noble.
Caca. Your mistress by the way?
Estif. My natural mistress.
Upon these jewels, sir, they're fair and rich,
And view 'em right.
Caca. To doubt 'em is an heresy.
Estif. A thousand ducats; 'tis upon necessity
Of present use; her husband, sir, is stubborn.
Caca. Long may he be so.
Estif. She desires withal
A better knowledge of your parts and person,
And when you please to do her so much honour——
Caca. Come let's dispatch.
Estif. In truth I've heard her say, sir,
Of a fat man she has not seen a sweeter.
But in this business, sir.
Caca. Let's do it first,
And then dispute; the lady's use may long for't.
Estif. All secrecy she would desire. She told me
How wise you are.
Caca. We are not wise to talk thus.
Carry her the gold, I'll look her out a jewel
Shall sparkle like her eyes, and thee another.
Come, pr'ythee come, I long to serve the lady;
Long monstrously. Now, valour, I shall meet ye,
You that dare dukes.
" *Estif.* Green goose, you are now in sippets."
[*Exeunt.*

SCENE II.

A Chamber. Enter the Duke, SANCHIO, JUAN, *and* ALONZO.

Duke. He shall not have his will, I shall prevent him.
I have a toy here that will turn the tide,
And suddenly and strangely. Here, Don Juan,
Do you present it to him.

Juan. I am commanded. [*Exit.*

Duke. A fellow founded out of charity,
" And moulded to the height, contemn his maker,
" Curb the free hand that fram'd him!"
It must not be.

San. That such an oyster-shell should hold a pearl,
And of so rare a price, in prison!
" Was she made to be the matter of her own undoing,
" To let a slovenly unwieldy fellow,
" Unruly and self-will'd, dispose her beauties?
" We suffer all, sir, in this sad eclipse;
" She should shine, where she might show like herself,
" An absolute sweetness, to comfort those admire her,
" And shed her beams upon her friends.
" We are gull'd all,
" And all the world will grumble at your patience,
" If she be ravish'd thus."

Duke. Ne'er fear it, Sanchio;
We'll have her free again, and move at court
In her clear orb. But one sweet handsomeness
To bless this part of Spain, and have that slubber'd!

Alon. 'Tis every good man's cause, and we must stir in it.

Duke. I'll warrant ye, he shall be glad to please us,
" And glad to share too; we shall hear anon
" A new song from him; let's attend a little."
[*Exeunt.*

SCENE III.

Another Chamber. Enter LEON *and* JUAN *with a Commission.*

Leon. Col'nel, I am bound to you for this nobleness.
I should have been your officer, 'tis true, sir;
And a proud man I should have been to've serv'd you.
'T has pleas'd the king, out of his boundless favours,
To make me your companion: this commission
Gives me a troop of horse.

Juan. I do rejoice at it,
And am a glad man we shall gain your company.
I'm sure the king knows you are newly married,
And out of that respect gives you more time, sir.

Leon. Within four days I'm gone, so he commands me,
And 'tis not mannerly for me to argue it.
The time grows shorter still—Are your goods ready?

Juan. They are aboard.

Leon. Who waits there?

Enter Servant.

Ser. Sir.

Leon. Do you hear, ho? Go carry this unto your mistress, sir,
And let her see how much the king has honour'd me;
Bid her be lusty, she must make a soldier.
Go, take down all the hangings,
And pack up all my cloaths, my plate and jewels,
And all the furniture that's portable.
Sir, when we lie in garrison, 'tis necessary
We keep a handsome port, for the king's honour.
And, do your hear? let all your lady's wardrobe
Be safely placed in trunks; they must along too.

Ser. Whither must they go, sir?

Leon. To the wars, Lorenzo.

Ser. Must my mistress go, sir?

Leon. Ay, your mistress, and you, and all must go.
I will not leave a turnspit behind me
" That has one dram of spleen against a Dutchman:"
All must go.

Ser. Why Pedro, Vasco, Diego, come, help me, boys. [*Exit.*

Juan. H'as taken a brave way to save his honour,
" And cross the duke; now I shall love him dearly."
By the life of credit thou'rt a noble gentleman.

Enter MARGARITTA, *led by two Ladies.*

Leon. Why how now, wife; what, sick at my preferment?
This is not kindly done.

Mar. No sooner love ye,
Love ye entirely, sir, brought to consider
The goodness of your mind and mine own duty,
But lose you instantly, be divorc'd from ye!
This is a cruelty. I'll to the king,
And tell him 'tis unjust to part two souls,
Two minds so nearly mix'd.

Leon. By no means, sweat-heart.

Mar. If he were married but four days, as I am—

Leon. He'd hang himself the fifth, or fly his country. [*Aside.*

Mar. He'd make it treason for that tongue that durst
But talk of war, or any thing to vex him.
You shall not go.

Leon. Indeed I must, sweet wife.
What, should I lose the king for a few kisses?
We'll have enough.

Mar. I'll to the duke, my cousin; he shall to th' king.

Leon. He did me this great office;
I thank his grace for't: should I pray him now
T'undo't again? Fie, 'twere a base discredit.

Mar. Would I were able, sir, to bear you company;
How willing should I be then, and how merry!
I will not live alone.

Leon. Be in peace, you shall, not. [*Knocking within.*

Mar. What knocking's this? Oh, Heaven, my head! Why, rascal,
I think the wars begun i'the house already.

Leon. The preparation is, they're taking down

And packing up the hangings, plate, and jewels,
And all those furnitures that shall befit me
When I lie in garrison.

Enter LORENZO.

Lor. Must the coach go to, sir?
Leon. How will your lady pass to the sea else easily?
We shall find shipping for't there to transport it.
Mar. I go? Alas!
Leon. I'll have a main care of ye:
I know you are sickly, he shall drive the easier,
And all accommodation shall attend ye.
Mar. Would I were able.
Leon. Come, I warrant ye.
Am not I with ye, sweet? Are her clothes packt up,
And all her linen? Give your maids direction:
You know my time's but short, and I'm commanded.
Mar. Let me have a nurse,
And all such necessary people with me;
An easy bark.
Leon. It shall not trot, I warrant ye;
Curvet it may sometimes.
Mar. I am with child, sir.
Leon. At four days warning! This is something speedy.
Do you conceive as our jennets do, with a west-wind?
My heir will be an errant fleet one, lady.
" I'll swear you was a maid when I first lay with ye.
" *Mar.* Pray do not swear. I thought I was a maid too:

" But we may both be cozen'd in that point, sir.
" *Leon.* In such a strait point, sure I could not err, madam.
" *Juan.* This is another tenderness to try him.
" Fetch her up now."
Mar. You must provide a cradle, and what a trouble's that!
Leon. The sea shall rock it;
'Tis the best nurse; 'twill roar and rock together.
A swinging storm will sing you such a lullaby!
Mar. Faith let me stay: I shall but shame you, sir.
Leon. An you were a thousand shames you shall along with me:
At home I'm sure you'd prove a million.
Every man carries the bundle of his sins
Upon his back: you are mine; I'll sweat for ye.

Enter Duke, ALONZO, *and* SANCHIO.

Duke. What, sir, preparing for your noble journey?
'Tis well, and full of care.
I saw your mind was wedded to the war,
And knew you'd prove some good man for your country;
Therefore, fair cousin, with your gentle pardon,
I got this place. What, mourn at his advancement!
You are to blame; he'll come again, sweet cousin:
Meantime, like sad Penelope and sage,
Among your maids at home, and housewifely—
Leon. No, sir, I dare not leave her to that solitariness:
She's young, and grief or ill news from those quarters,
May daily cross her: she shall go along, sir.

Duke. By no means, captain.

Leon. By all means, an't please ye.

Duke. What, take a young and tender-body'd lady,
And expose her to those dangers, and those tumults!
A sickly lady too!

Leon. 'Twill make her well, sir;
There's no such friend to health as wholesome travel.

San. Away, it must not be.

Alon. It ought not, sir.
Go hurry her! It is not humane, captain.

Duke. I cannot blame her tears——Fright her with tempests,
With thunder of the war!
I dare swear if she were able——

Leon. She's most able:
And, pray ye, swear not: she must go, there's no remedy:
Nor greatness, nor the trick you had to part us,
Which smells too rank, too open, too evident,
Shall hinder me. Had she but ten hours life,
Nay less, but two hours, I would have her with me;
I would not leave her fame to so much ruin,
To such a desolation and discredit, as
Her weakness and your hot will wou'd work her to.
Fie, fie, for shame!

Enter PEREZ.

What mask is this now?
More tropes and figures to abuse my suff'rance!
What cousin's this?

Juan. Michael Van Owle, how dost thou?
In what dark barn, or tod of aged ivy,
Hast thou lain hid?
Per. Things must both ebb and flow, colonel,
And people must conceal and shine again.
You're welcome hither, as your friend may say, gentlemen;
A pretty house, ye see, handsomely seated,
Sweet and convenient walks, the waters crystal.
Alon. He's certain mad.
Juan. As mad as a French taylor, that
Has nothing in his head but ends of fustians.
Per. I see you're packing now, my gentle cousin,
And my wife told me I should find it so;
'Tis true I do: you were merry when I was last here;
But 'twas your will to try my patience, madam.
I'm sorry that my swift occasions
Can let you take your pleasure here no longer;
Yet I would have you think, my honoured cousin,
This house, and all I have, are all your servants.
Leon. What house, what pleasure, sir? what do you mean?
Per. You hold the jest so stiff, 'twill prove discourteous.
This house, I mean; the pleasures of this place.
Leon. And what of them?
Per. They're mine, sir, and you know it:
My wife's, I mean, and so conferr'd upon me.
The hangings, sir, I must entreat your servants,
That are so busy in their offices,

Again to minister to their right uses.
I shall take view o' th' plate anon, and furnitures
That are of under place. You're merry still, cousin,
And of a pleasant constitution:
Men of great fortunes make their mirths *ad placitum.*

Leon. Pr'ythee, good stubborn wife, tell me directly;
Good evil wife, leave fooling, and tell me honestly,
Is this my kinsman?

Mar. I can tell ye nothing.

Leon. I've many kinsmen, but so mad a one,
And so fantastic——all the house?

Per. All mine,
And all within it. I will not bate you an ace on't.
Can't you receive a noble courtesy,
And quietly and handsomely as ye ought, coz,
But you must ride o' the top on't?

Leon. Canst thou fight?

Per. I'll tell ye presently? I could have done, sir.

Leon. For you must law and claw before ye get it.

Juan. Away, no quarrels.

Leon. Now I am more temperate,
I'll have it prov'd you were ne'er yet in Bedlam;
Never in love, for that's a lunacy;
No great 'state left ye, that ye never look'd for,
Nor cannot manage, that's a rank distemper;
That you were christen'd, and who answered for you,
And then I yield——*Do but look at him.*

Per. He has half persuaded me I was bred i'th' moon:
I have ne'er a brush at my breech—Are not we both
mad?

And is not this a fantastic house we are in,
And all a dream we do? Will you walk out?
And if I do not beat thee presently
Into a sound belief as sense can give thee,
Brick me into that wall there for a chimney-piece,
And say, I was one o' th' Cæsars done by a seal-cutter.

Leon. I'll talk no more; come, we'll away immediately.

Mar. Why then the house is his, and all that's in it:
I'll give away my skin, but I'll undo ye:
I gave it to his wife. You must restore, sir;
And make a new provision.

Per. Am I mad, now,
Or am I christen'd? You, my Pagan cousin,
My mighty Mahound kinsman, what quirk now?
You shall be welcome all. I hope to see, sir,
Your grace here, and my coz: we are all soldiers,
And must do naturally for one another.

Duke. Are you blank at this? Then I must tell ye, sir,
Ye've no command; now you may go at pleasure,
And ride your ass troop. " 'Twas a trick I used
" To try your jealousy, upon entreaty,
" And saving of your wife."

Leon. All this not moves me,
Nor stirs my gall, nor alters my affections.
You have more furniture, more houses, lady,
And rich ones too; I will make bold with those;
And you have land i' th' Indies, as I take it;
Thither we'll go, and view a while those climates,

Visit your factors there, that may betray ye.
'Tis done, we must go.
Mar. Now thou'rt a brave gentleman;
And by this sacred light I love thee dearly. Hark ye, sir,
The house is none of yours; I did but jest, sir;
You are no coz of mine; I beseech ye, vanish.
" I tell you plain, you have no more right than he
" Has, that senseless thing. Your wife has once more fool'd ye, sir.
" Go ye and consider."
Leon. Good-morrow, my sweet Mahound cousin.
You are welcome—welcome all—my cousin too—
We are soldiers, and should naturally do for one another.
Per. By this hand she dies for't,
Or any man that speaks for her.
" These are fine toys." [*Exit* Perez.
Mar. Let me request you stay but one poor month;
You shall have a commission, and I'll go too.
Give me but will so far.
Leon. Well, I will try ye.
Good-morrow to your grace; we've private business.
" *Duke.* If I miss thee again, I'm an arrant bungler.
" *Juan.* Thou shalt have my command, and I'll march under thee,
" Nay, be thy boy, before thou shalt be baffled;
" Thou art so brave a fellow.
" *Alon.* I have seen visions." [*Exeunt.*

ACT V. SCENE I.

MARGARITTA's *House.* *Enter* LEON, *with a letter, and* MARGARITTA.

" *Leon.*

" COME hither, wife. Do you know this hand?

" *Mar.* I do, sir; 'tis Estifania's, that was once my woman.

" *Leon.* She writes to me here, that one Cacafogo,
" An usuring jeweller's son, I know the rascal,
" Is mortally fallen in love with you.

" *Mar.* He is a monster; deliver me from mountains.

" *Leon.* Do you go a birding for all sorts of people?
" And this evening will come to ye, and shew ye jewels,
" And offers any thing to get access to you.
" If I can make or sport or profit on him,
" (For he is fit for both) she bids me use him,
" And so I will. Be you conformable, and follow but my will.

" *Mar.* I shall not fail, sir.

" *Leon.* Will the duke come again, do you think?

" *Mar.* No, sure, sir.
" H'as now no policy to bring him hither.

" *Leon.* Nor bring you to him, if my wit hold, fair wife.
" Let's in to dinner." [*Exeunt.*

SCENE II.

A Street. *Enter* PEREZ.

Per. Had I but lungs enough to bawl sufficiently,
That all the queans in Christendom might hear me,
That men might run away from the contagion,
I had my wish. Would it were made high treason,
Most infinite high, for any man to marry;
I mean, for a man that would live handsomely,
And like a gentleman in's wits and credit.
What torments shall I put her to? "Phalaris' bull now?
" Pox! they love bulling too well, tho' they smoke for't."
Cut her in pieces, every piece will live still,
And every morsel of her will do mischief.
They have so many lives, there's no hanging of 'em;
They are too light to drown, they're cork and feathers;
To burn too cold, they live like salamanders:
Under huge heaps of stones to bury her,
And so depress her as they did the giants,
She will move under more than built old Babel.
I must destroy her.

Enter CACAFOGO, *with a casket.*

Caca. Be cozen'd by a thing of clouts! a she moth,
That every silkman's shop breeds! To be cheated,
And of a thousand ducats, by a whim-wham!

Per. Who's that is cheated? Speak again, thou vision.

But art thou cheated? Minister some comfort.
Tell me, I conjure thee, "art thou cheated bravely?
"Come, pr'ythee come; art thou so pure a coxcomb,
"To be undone? Do not dissemble with me."

Caca. Then keep thy circle:
For I'm a spirit wild that flies about thee;
And, whosoe'er thou art, if thou be'st human,
I'd let thee plainly know, I'm cheated damnably.

Per. Ha, ha, ha!

Caca. Dost thou laugh? Damnably, I say, most damnably.

Per. By whom, good spirit? Speak, speak! Ha, ha, ha!

Caca. I'll utter; laugh till thy lungs crack; by a rascal woman!
"A lewd, abominable, and plain woman!"
Dost thou laugh still?

Per. I must laugh, pr'ythee pardon me,
I shall laugh terribly.

Caca. I shall be angry,
Terribly angry; I have cause.

Per. That's it;
And 'tis no reason but thou shouldst be angry,
Angry at heart; yet I must laugh still at thee.
By a woman cheated! Art sure it was a woman?

Caca. I shall break thy head; my valour itches at thee.

Per. It is no matter. By a woman cozen'd,
A real woman!

Caca. By a real devil.
Plague of her jewels, and her copper chains,
How rank they smell.

Per. Sweet, cozen'd sir, let's see them.
I have been cheated too, I would have you note that;
And lewdly cheated, by a woman also,
A scurvy woman. I am undone, sweet sir,
Therefore I must have leave to laugh.
Caca. Pray ye take it;
You are the merriest undone man in Europe.
What need we fiddles, bawdy songs, and sherry,
When our own miseries can make us merry?
Per. Ha, ha, ha!
I've seen these jewels: what a notable pennyworth
Have you had! You will not take, sir,
Some twenty ducats—
Caca. Thou'rt deceiv'd; I will take——
" *Per.* To clear your bargain, now.
" *Caca.* I'll take some ten,"
Some any thing, some half ten, half a ducat.
Per. An excellent lapidary set these stones, sure:
D'ye mark their waters?
Caca. Quicksand choak their waters,
And her's that brought them too: but I shall find her.
Per. And so shall I, I hope; but do not hurt her.
" If you had need of cozening, as you may have,
" (For such gross natures will desire it often,
" 'Tis, at sometimes too, a fine variety)"
You cannot find in all this kingdom,
A woman that can cozen ye so neatly.
She has taken half mine anger off with this trick. [*Exit.*
Caca. If I were valiant now, I'd kill this fellow.
I've money enough lies by me, at a pinch,

To pay for twenty rascals lives that vex me.
I'll to this lady; there I shall be satisfied. [*Exit.*

SCENE III.

A Street. Enter PEREZ *and* ESTIFANIA, *meeting.*

Per. Why, how dar'st thou meet me again, thou rebel,
And know'st how thou hast us'd me thrice, thou rascal?
Were there not ways enough to fly my vengeance,
No holes nor vaults to hide thee from my fury,
But thou must meet me face to face to kill thee?
I would not seek thee to destroy thee willingly,
But now thou com'st t' invite me, com'st upon me.
How like a sheep-biting rogue, taken i' the manner,
And ready for a halter, dost thou look now?
Thou hast a hanging look, thou scurvy thing!
Hast ne'er a knife,
Nor e'er a string to lead thee to Elysium?
Be there no pitiful 'pothecaries in this town,
That have compassion upon wretched women,
That dare administer a dram of ratsbane,
But thou must fall to me?

Estif. I know you've mercy.

Per. If I had tons of mercy thou deserv'st none.
What new tricks now a-foot, and what new houses
Have you i' the air? What orchards in apparition?
What can'st thou say for thy life?

Estif. Little or nothing.

I know you'll kill me, and I know 'tis useless
To beg for mercy. Pray let me draw my book out,
And pray a little.

Per. Do, a very little;
For I have farther business than thy killing.
I have money yet to borrow. Speak when you're ready.

Estif. Now, now, sir, now [*Shews a pistol.*
Come on. Do you start off from me?
Do you sweat, great captain? Have you seen a spirit?

Per. Do you wear guns?

Estif. I am a soldier's wife, sir,
And by that privilege I may be arm'd.
Now, what's the news? And let's discourse more friendly,
And talk of our affairs in peace.

Per. Let me see,
Pr'ythee let me see thy gun; 'tis a very pretty one.

Estif. No, no, sir, you shall feel.

Per. Hold, hold, ye villain! what, would you
Kill your own husband?

Estif. Let mine own husband then,
Be in's own wits. There, there's a thousand ducats.
Who must provide for you? And yet you'll kill me.

Per. I will not hurt thee for ten thousand millions.

Estif. When will you redeem your jewels? I have pawn'd 'em,
You see for what we must keep touch.

Per. I'll kiss thee;
And get as many more, I'll make thee famous.
Had we the house now!

Estif. Come along with me;
If that be vanish'd, there be more to hire, sir.
Per. I see I am an ass when thou art near me.
[*Exeunt.*

SCENE IV.

A Chamber. Enter LEON *and* MARGARITTA.

Leon. Come, we'll away unto your country house,
And there we'll learn to live contentedly.
This place is full of charge, and full of hurry;
No part of sweetness dwells about these cities,
Mar. Whither you will, I wait upon your pleasure:
Live in a hollow tree, sir, I'll live with ye.
Leon. Ay, now you strike a harmony, a true one,
When your obedience waits upon your husband. 161
Why, now I doat upon you, love ye dearly;
And my rough nature falls, like roaring streams,
Clearly and sweetly into your embraces.
Oh, what a jewel is a woman excellent,
A wise, a virtuous, and a noble woman!
" When we meet such, we bear our stamps on both sides,
" And through the world we hold our current virtues.
" Alone we are single medals, only faces,
" And wear our fortunes out in useless shadows."
Command you now, and ease me of that trouble;
I'll be as humble to you as a servant.
Bid whom you please, invite your noble friends,

They shall be welcome all, now experience
Has bound you fast unto the chain of goodness.
[*Clashing swords, a cry within.*] Down with their swords!
What noise is this? what dismal cry?
Mar. 'Tis loud too.
Sure there's some mischief done i' th' street; look out there.
Leon. Look out, and help.

Enter a Servant.

Ser. Oh, sir, the duke Medina——
Leon. What of the duke Medina?
Ser. Oh, sweet gentleman is almost slain!
Mar. Away, away, and help him;
All the house help. [*Exit Servant.*
Leon. How! slain? Why, Margaritta,
Wife, sure some new device they have a-foot again,
Some trick upon my credit; I shall meet it.
I'd rather guide a ship imperial,
Alone, and in a storm, than rule one woman.

Enter Duke, SANCHIO, ALONZO, *and Servant.*

Mar. How came you hurt, sir?
Duke. I fell out with my friend, the noble colonel.
My cause was naught, for 'twas about your honour;
And he that wrongs the innocent ne'er prospers,
" And he has left me thus;" for charity,
Lend me a bed to ease my tortur'd body,
That ere I perish I may shew my penitence.
I fear I'm slain.

Leon. Help, gentlemen, to carry him.
There shall be nothing in this house, my lord,
But as your own.

Duke. I thank ye, noble sir.

Leon. To bed with him; and, wife, give your attendance.

[*Exeunt Duke,* San. Alon. Marg. *and Servant.*

Enter JUAN.

Leon. Afore me,
'Tis rarely counterfeited.

Juan. True, it is so, sir?
" And take you heed this last blow do not spoil ye."
He is not hurt, only we made a scuffle,
As tho' we purpos'd anger: that same scratch,
On's hand he took, to colour all, and draw compassion,
That he might get into your house more cunningly.
I must not stay; stand now, and you're a brave fellow,

Leon. I thank ye, noble colonel, and I honour ye.
Never be quiet! [*Exit* Juan.

Enter MARGARITTA.

Mar. He's most desperate ill, sir;
I do not think these ten months will recover him.

Leon. Does he hire my house to play the fool in,
Or does it stand on fairy ground? We're haunted.
Are all men and their wives troubled with dreams thus?

Mar. What ail you, sir?

Leon. Nay, what ail you, sweet wife,
To put these daily pastimes on my patience?

What dost thou see in me, that I should suffer this?
" Have I not done my part like a true husband,
" And paid some desperate debts you never look'd for?
" *Mar.* You have done handsomely, I must confess, sir.
" *Leon.* Have I not kept thee waking like a hawk,
" And watch'd thee with delights, to satisfy thee,
" The very tithes of which had won a widow?"
Mar. Alas, I pity ye,
Leon. Thou'lt make me angry;
Thou never saw'st me mad yet.
Mar. You are always;
You carry a kind of bedlam still about ye.
Leon. If thou pursu'st me farther, I run stark mad.
If you have more hurt dukes, or gentlemen,
To lie here on your cure, I shall be desperate.
I know the trick, and you shall feel I know it,
Are ye so hot that no hedge can contain ye?
I'll have thee let blood in all the veins about thee;
I'll have thy thoughts found too, and have them open'd,
Thy spirits purg'd, for those are they that fire ye.
The maid shall be thy mistress, thou the maid,
And all her servile labours thou shalt reach at,
And go through cheerfully, or else sleep empty,
That maid shall lie by me, to teach you duty;
You in a pallet by, to humble ye,
And grieve for what you lose, *thou foolish, wicked woman.*
Mar. I've lost myself, sir,
And all that was my base self, disobedience: [*Kneels.*

My wantonness, my stubbornness I've lost too.
And now, by that pure faith good wives are crown'd with,
By your own nobleness——

Leon. *Beware, beware——have you no fetch now?*

Mar. *No, by my repentance, no.*

Leon. *And art thou truly, truly honest?*

Mar. *These tears will shew it.*

Leon. I take you up, and wear you next my heart:
See you be worth it.——

Enter ALTEA.

Now, what with you?

Alt. I come to tell my lady,
There is a fulsome fellow would fain speak wih her.

Leon. 'Tis Cacafogo; keep him from the duke,
The duke from him; anon he'll yield us laughter.

Alt. *Where is it, please you, that we shall detain him?*
He seems at war with reason, full of wine.

Leon. *To the cellar with him; 'tis the drunkard's den,*
Fit cover for such beasts. Should he be resty,
Say I'm at home; unwieldy as he is,
He'll creep into an augre-hole to shun me.

Alt. *I'll dispose him there.* [Exit.

Leon. Now, Margaritta, comes your trial on:
The duke expects you; acquit yourself to him;
I put you to the test; you have my trust,
My confidence, my love.

Mar. I will deserve 'em. [*Exit.*

Leon. *My work is done, and now my heart's at ease.*

I read in ev'ry look, she means me fairly;
And nobly shall my love reward her for't.
He who betrays his rights, the husband's rights,
To pride and wantonness; or who denies
Affection to the heart he has subdu'd,
Forfeits his claim to manhood and humanity. [Exit.

---

* *SCENE V.*

A Chamber. Duke discovered in a Night-gown.

Duke. Why, now this is most excellent invention.
I shall succed, spite of this huffing husband.
I can but smile to think most wary spouses
The soonest are deceiv'd.

Enter MARGARITTA.

Who's there? My love?

Mar. 'Tis I, my lord.

Duke. Are you alone, sweet friend?

Mar. Alone, and come to enquire how your wounds are.

Duke. I have none, lady; not a hurt about me;
My damages I did but counterfeit,
And feign'd the quarrel to enjoy you, lady.
I am as lusty and as full of health,
As high in blood——

* This scene is entirely altered for representation; as there was no possibility of distinguishing the variations from the original, it was thought necessary to omit it in order to prevent confusion.

Mar. As low in blood, you mean:
Dishonest thoughts debase the greatest birth;
The man that acts unworthily, tho' ennobled,
Sullies his honour.

Duke. Nay, nay, my Margaritta;
Come to my couch, and there let's lisp love's language.

Mar. Would you take that which I've no right to give?
Steal wedlock's property; and in his house,
Beneath the roof of him that entertains you,
Would you his wife betray?—Will you become
Th' ungrateful viper, who, restor'd to life,
Venom'd the breast which sav'd him?

Duke. Leave these dull thoughts to mortifying penance;
Let us, while love is lusty, prove its power.

Mar. Ill wishes, once, my lord, my mind debas'd:
You found my weakness, wanted to ensnare it:
Shameful, I own my fault, but 'tis repented.
No more the wanton Margaritta now,
But the chaste wife of Leon. His great merit,
His manly tenderness, his noble nature,
Commands from me affection in return,
Pure as esteem can offer. He has won me;
I owe him all my heart.

Duke. Indeed, fair lady,
This jesting well becomes a sprightly beauty.
Love prompts to celebrate sublimer rights.
No more memento's; let me press you to me,
And stifle with my kisses——

Mar. Nay, then, within, there!

Enter LEON, JUAN, ALONZO, *and* SANCHIO.

Leon. *Did you call, my wife; or you, my lord?*
Was it your grace that wanted me?—No answer!
How do you, my good lord? *What, out of bed!*
Methinks you look but poorly on this matter.
Has my wife wounded you? You were well before.
Duke. *More hurt than ever; spare your reproach;*
I feel too much already.
Leon. *I see it sir—And now your grace shall know,*
I can as readily pardon as revenge.
Be comforted; all is forgotten.
Duke. *I thank you, sir.*
Leon. Wife, you are a right one;
And now, with unknown nations I dare trust ye.
Juan. No more feign'd fights, my lord, they never prosper.

Enter LORENZO.

Lor. *Please you, sir.*
We cannot keep this gross fat man in order:
He swears he'll have admittance to my lady,
And reels about and clamours most outrageously.
Leon. *Let him come up—Wife, here's another suitor*
We forgot; h'as been sighing in the cellar,
Making my casks his mistresses.
Will your grace permit us to produce a rival?
Duke. *No more on that theme, I request, Don Leon.*

Leon. Here comes the porpus; he's devilish drunk. Let me stand by.

Enter CACAFOGO *drunk.*

Caca. *Where is my* bona roba? *Oh, you're all here. Why, I don't fear snap-dragons—Impotential, powerfully potion'd—I can drink with Hector, and beat him too. Then what care I for captains; I'm full of Greek wine; the true, ancient courage.—Sweet Mrs. Margaritta, let me kiss thee —Your kisses shall pay me for his kicking.*

Leon. *What would you?*

Caca. *Sir!*

Leon. *Lead off the wretch.*

Duke. *Most filthy figure, truly.*

Caca. *Filthy! Oh, you're a prince; yet I can buy all of you, your wives and all.*

Juan. *Sleep, and be silent.*

Caca. *Speak you to your creditors, good Captain Half-pay;*
I'll not take thy pawn in.

Leon. Which of the butts is thy mistress?

Caca. Butt in thy belly.

Leon. There are two in thine, I'm sure, it is grown so monstrous,

Caca. Butt in thy face.

Leon. Go, carry him to sleep; [*Exit* Caca.
When he is sober, let him out to rail,
Or hang himself; there will be no loss of him.

Enter PEREZ *and* ESTIFANIA

Leon. Who's this; my Mahound cousin?

Per. Good sir, 'tis very good: would I'd a house too,
For there's no talking in the open air.
You have a pretty seat, you have the luck on't,
A pretty lady too, I have miss'd both;
My carpenter built in a mist, I thank him.
Do me the courtesy to let me see it,
See it once more. But I shall cry for anger.
I'll hire a chandler's shop close under ye,
And for my foolery, sell soap and whip-cord.
Nay, if you do not laugh now, and laugh heartily,
You are a fool, coz.

Leon. I must laugh a little;
And now I've done. Coz, thou shalt live with me,
My merry coz, the world shall not divorce us:
Thou art a valiant man, and thou shalt never want.
Will this content thee?

Per. I'll cry, and then be thankful,
Indeed I will, and I'll be honest to ye;
I'd live a swallow here, I must confess.
Wife, I forgive thee all if thou be honest,
And at thy peril, I believe thee excellent.

Estif. If I prove otherwise, let me beg first.

Mar. Hold, this is yours, some recompence for service,
Use it to nobler ends than he that gave it.

Duke. And this is yours, your true commission, sir.
Now you're a captain.

Leon. You're a noble prince, sir;
And now a soldier.

Juan. Sir, I shall wait upon you through all fortunes.

Alon. And I.

Alt. And I must needs attend my mistress.

Leon. Will you go, sister?

Alt. Yes, indeed, good brother:
I have two ties, mine own blood, and my mistress.

Mar. Is she your sister?

Leon. Yes, indeed, good wife,
And my best sister, for she prov'd so, wench,
When she deceiv'd you with a loving husband.

Alt. I would not deal so truly for a stranger.

Mar. Well, I could chide ye, but it must be lovingly,
And like a sister.
I'll bring you on your way, and feast ye nobly,
For now I have an honest heart to love ye,
And then deliver you to the blue Neptune.

Juan. Your colours you must wear, and wear 'em proudly,
Wear 'em before the bullet, and in blood too.
And all the world shall know we're virtue's servants.

Duke. And all the world shall know, a noble mind
Makes women beautiful, and envy blind.

Leon. All you who mean to lead a happy life,
First learn to rule, and then to have a wife.

EPILOGUE.

GOOD night, our worthy friends, and may you part
Each with as merry and as free a heart
As you came hither. To those noble eyes,
That deign to smile on our poor faculties,
And give a blessing to our labouring ends,
As we hope many to such fortune sends
Their own desires, wives fair as light, as chaste:
To those that live by spite, wives made in haste.

Printed in Great Britain
by Amazon